Mandela Effect

TS Caladan

2019, TWB Press
www.twbpress.com

"As a child, I knew there was magic in the world. I grew up to find good magic gone and only Black Magic remained."

~ tsc

Edited by TS Caladan

Cover Art by TS Caladan

Published by TWB Press, Centennial, Colorado

ISBN: 978-1-944045-62-3

WARNING

FEDERAL LAW ALLOWS CITIZENS TO
REPRODUCE, DISTRIBUTE, OR EXHIBIT
PORTIONS OF COPYRIGHTED MOTION
PICTURES, VIDEO TAPES, OR VIDEO
DISCS UNDER CERTAIN CIRCUMSTANCES
WITHOUT AUTHORIZATION OF THE
COPYRIGHT HOLDER.

THIS INFRINGEMENT OF COPYRIGHT IS
CALLED "FAIR USE" AND IS ALLOWED
FOR PURPOSES OF CRITICISM, NEWS
REPORTING, TEACHING, AND PARODY.

CONTENTS

* Introduction to the Mandela Effect

Think you know reality? Think you know somewhat of how the universe works? How about your memories? Are they intact? Have they been wiped or altered in any way? Would you know? Do your memories suddenly differ greatly from others around you? Or how about the world physically, unnaturally (almost magically) *changing* and we've hardly noticed? Couldn't happen, huh? Like CERN or someone screwing with Time-Machines? And then, what you thought you knew of the world has changed a little or a lot. But not to everyone.

People, today, have completely different views of recent and old events and what was once an unshakable, solid, constant reality we all shared and remembered. This is not the normal mistaken memories of the misinformed or the ignorant. This is UNNATURAL, inexplicable changes and not the usual ones as a result of time passing. Now things are very different, physically, than the way they were. *(And they shouldn't be)*. This will be proven to you when you take a Mandela Test and review the evidence in this book. Before the Mandela Effect, no one had ever questioned such things as:

* Did the large pyramids at Giza switch positions?
* Do the Moon and Mars seem different than they were?
* Have countries changed borders and sizes as well as whole continents shifted, seemingly overnight? Have U.S. states changed shape?
* Has history changed with new events no one remembers, while other memories have vanished? Were there earlier, advanced technologies shown in photos and films, previously unknown?
* Have giant statues, monuments, ancient ruins and odd buildings suddenly come into existence?
* Did the Statue of Liberty move from Ellis Island to Liberty Island?
* Have well-known statues and works of art altered?

* Have classic lines in films and famous lyrics in songs, we all know, *changed?* Have disks, tapes, books and various Media on our shelves changed lately?
* Do names, logos, signs, designs and packaging of well-known products appear *different* than the way most remember?
* Have words instantly changed their spelling and also the names of famous people, as if by magic?
* Have new/strange animals, plants and other unfamiliar bits of nature suddenly appeared as if they've always been around?
* Have our bodies changed, organs in different places and different sizes with slightly different arrangements than before?

The KJV Bibles, everywhere, have undeniably changed and it is not a matter of debate.

None of this, and far more than you can imagine, would ever have been questioned, considered or have really happened, before the Mandela Effect - Wave - frequency - vibration HIT.

There will be such *war* when Mandela surfaces on the mainstream, which is inevitable, already the subject of books, articles, videos, etc. Already, there is the division between believers and debunkers. Enemies of truth own the public Media channels and will certainly ridicule Mandela people in attempts to explain the phenomenon, by reporting it's only a *lunacy craze* and nothing strange is happening. The power of 'suggestion.' Passing on false rumors. "These wackos must have Alzheimer's disease."

The war is on!

DO NOT BELIEVE THE DEFINITION OF THE MANDELA EFFECT~

(If your definition is 'mistaken memories'? Investigation will show, that's not true).

Fiona Broome (witch's broom?) launched a website in 2009 after she discovered during a convention that many people have different views of what happened to Nelson Mandela. History records he was imprisoned in the 1980s. Many believed he'd died in prison while others (in the majority) agreed with history: Nelson Mandela was certainly released, became a global hero and eventually the President of South Africa. She blogged the question and found many people with divergent views, and they were certain of their views. Skeptics would claim Ms. Broome found numerous *not very intelligent* people who were clueless and couldn't pass History 101. But...

People started to LOOK at the world closer. The more they searched, the more they discovered that our reality and existence itself simply *does not add up. Not anymore.* From 2011 on, and primarily in the last couple of years, the Effect and videos by researchers have gone viral. M.E. has exploded on YT as more evidence has entered our consciousness...

And it blows most people's minds!

Skeptics will always 'bury their head in sand,' 'put blinders on' or close their eyes to the 'unicorn in the room.' Doesn't matter how much real, concrete, physical evidence you present to them, they will never admit there's a 'unicorn in the room.' What if more and more people see the impossible unicorn? Who's crazy then? What have simple people always done when confronted by an alien or a contradiction they do not understand? They usually deny it, want to stamp it out, fear it, run from it or call you a "fool" for believing in something more than they believe. Don't be simple, be complex.

Basically, there are two kinds of people: 1) Those who believe there's magic in the world. 2) Those who are confident *there is no magic in the world.* Or, those who think a blade of grass can unnaturally change and others who are sure that it is impossible. We believe what has FOUNDATION to us, what seems sensible and toss "absurdities" into the Fantasy Bin. Maybe we have the wrong Foundations? The wrong, narrow education? Possibly. To understand the truth or what's really going on...

You need lessons in Science "Fiction"? It's not fantasy. Predictive Programming. Elites, who control our Media and "entertainment," have been telling us about what they've planned (Mandela) for a long time. Some of us are only realizing this now. Maybe our fundamental education and experiences should have included SF stories that inspired us to fly in dreams, to the furthest reaches of the Imagination? Outer Limits? Twilight Zones? That is, if you wanted to create, innovate, invent, mature or progress technically, mentally and spiritually? Grow and extend yourself outside of boxes, limits, and stop being "children."? To know or discover truth: We have to see beyond the surface of things in front of our eyes. It's always been that way, long before the Mandela

Wave struck and pushed us to the Dark Side, virtually overnight. Maybe they're doing this via technology they've kept from us, perverted Tesla Technology (they've done before)?

Maybe we should take a scientific approach? Be open? No fear. Because now, there truly are 'holes' in our world, in our logic, in our sense of what's real. *Is our universe an artificial Matrix?*

You can ease your mind and not believe in a fluid, unstable reality that might be morphing daily? Choose to *not* bother to check what the Mandela Community claims. I mean, why bother? It's a waste of the skeptic's time to look into the research or see for themselves because: "They know better. Nothing can supernaturally change. Magic doesn't exist. There's nothing to Mandela. People are just stupid, under delusions and have had it wrong for ages. These are not paradoxes or 100% impossibilities, contradictions where parallel worlds intersect or are in flux. No. People have different views of reality. They remember wrong lines, titles, song lyrics and there's nothing more to it."

Oh really? That's what an un-scientist might say. Be scientists. Use your eyes and ears. Search your feelings ("Luke"). Realize what is different right in front of you, when you look at a world map, when you walk down a street, when you shop in grocery stores and see altered signs and product labels on the shelves, etc. If you can?

The Effect is not a matter of people remembering *differently,* it is **the fact that the 'solid' reality of our timeline has suddenly changed!** The 'real' or old world we once knew is now gone and has been replaced with a simulation or a 'dark realm' that appears somewhat like what we knew, but is *completely different.* After you read this book, study and check the evidence, you might agree? But maybe you won't?

Let's discuss what are not Mandela Effects...

Real Mandela Effects are not false rumors like people believed Jerry Mathers (Beaver Cleaver) "died in Vietnam." No, he didn't. Or trivia, like Captain Kirk never said: "Beam me up, Scotty." It's true, always been true and not a Mandela Effect. Buttons and T-shirts at conventions contained the phrase, but it was never stated exactly that way in the original series. Take it from a long time Trekker. Always a slight variation was stated. You'll see (they say) that in 'Casablanca,' there's an M.E. Absolutely not true. Possibly there *will be* an Effect to mutate many of the classic lines, but "Play it again, Sam" was never said by Bogart. If you were well-acquainted with Hollywood trivia, you'd know this fact. It was always: "Play it, Sam. Play it, Sam."

Be skeptical, but then delve into 'Mandela' and see for yourself, openly, without prejudice. Many nature photos have been placed online that seem unreal. Photo-shopped? They could also be real. We don't know for sure and we certainly shouldn't believe them to be Mandela simply because they're online. But. New animals and landscapes now seem to be part of our physical world where they never were before. Evidence mounts, as in other departments, strange oddities appear to have "always been with us." "New histories." Really? Why is it we only noticed these anomalies (changes/differences) now or recently? Everything has to be investigated thoroughly before we *believe.*

The idea that new areas, islands, have appeared and new ancient sites are now a part of our physical world, previously unknown, is a very intriguing concept and will be examined.

I encourage you to YouTube the many findings/videos of Mandela researchers, but **don't believe everything**. I've researched space and ancient mysteries for almost 5 decades. I can safely say that a lot of space or ancient mystery Mandelas are semi-wrong: You haven't been informed of these things or they are old facts you're only finding out now. For example, there's always been ice at the lunar poles and a very thin lunar atmosphere and structures throughout the Solar System. Nothing new; you just haven't been told. How about there's now stone "hats" on the giant Easter Island statues? "It's a Mandela!" Nope. There has always been a row of stone giants with "hats" and a few with painted "eyes." The vast majority are hat-less. No changes here. People are not very well-educated. Sometimes.

False "Effects" must be realized. Do not go "crazy" and lump everything as a M.E. phenomenon. That goes for me, too. The phonies or false-memories or stupidity of people should not take away from real Mandelas, which are *absolutely astounding!* If I presented a UFO lecture and showed a hundred strange photos of unknown objects in the sky, I would have to say: "Don't believe it all." Many M.E.s are untrue. Or *planted there to be BS* by skeptic shills, paid to undermine the Mandela Movement?

I originally believed that the first Mandela Effect, the supposed first one that started it all, *was not a true Mandela.* I mean, surely we know Nelson Mandela did not die in prison. Right? After studying the evidence...I've changed my view. Worlds are colliding. I think it can be proved. I now know that at least one other parallel world exists; there could be an infinite number of similar universes? I've learned to not be so sure or insist that this is the way history flowed and such and such is definitely a fact. We cannot demand this one thing is true anymore or that stat is absolutely our history. Maybe, in another world, a completely different alternative happened? Maybe there's been crossovers?

It is not a case of companies updating/improving their logos or changing small details on packaging. M.E. investigators have checked these items, again and again, and companies report: "It's always been like that." See for yourself. It's not a case of studios changing famous lines in new film copies, or music recordings, different than old copies. In a lot of cases, the new reality completely clashes with what we remember...because **(POP!)** *some things that we remember well, do not exist anymore and never existed!?*

Once you investigate the real Mandelas, not very small product changes or obscure companies few remember, but famous line-changes in movies and lyrics of well-known songs, etc...

You will be shocked! There is extraordinary magic in the world now. *Black Magic!* Who's doing this to our reality, our timeline? Why? What will happen in future when more of our universe morphs and is thrust to the Dark Side? What is changing the world we've always trusted? Answers are in this book.

Share my "analysis of a worldwide phenomenon" with others. Have them take the Test and see what they remember? Do trivia questions. Of the questions, which item sounds familiar/correct and which one sounds odd and *can't* be the truth? Look up the present "facts," new spellings, etc. Check every single bit of information in this book and see for yourself. Decide. Have there been bizarre changes from what you remember? Google or YouTube our new world.

Surprise.

** Mandela Test Questions and Answers

Not a contest or real test to see if you're right or wrong because there is no right and wrong answers anymore. There is what was and what is now. The idea is not to get the correct or current answer, but to simply express: WHAT YOU REMEMBER. Which of the examples do you remember? Which sounds right and which sounds wrong?

Can you answer the following questions?

1. In the first two Star Wars films, did C3PO have a silver, lower leg?

❧ Like all lovers of sci-fi, old Star Trek and especially Star Wars, I have seen the films dozens of times. My eyes must have scanned millions of Star Wars images over decades and never did C3PO ever have a silver, right leg from the knee down. He does now. Look at the first two films and you'll see it's true. When the droid was in the desert with R2, when C3PO was in Lando's sky city in pieces in a box, there was the silver leg. Yet this is no one's memories. It's a recent development. Millions of people are not wrong in their memories of all-gold. Various SW books and parodies have not changed and show the droid as entirely gold. Every C3PO plastic model has not changed to the silver leg. How could official Star Wars merchandising, books and videos have gotten it completely wrong over decades? How could every other detail in C3PO's appearance be there, but everyone, EVERYONE, seems to have missed this? No way.

You'll hear producers of the new SW films say they "...Decided to no longer use the robot's silver leg" (like it's always been there?). *That's the Dark Side talking.* Millions of fans know better.

2. At the end of 'The Empire Strikes Back,' does Darth Vader say, "No, Luke. *I* am your father."? Or does he say, "No. *I* am your father."?

❧ There are many parodies of the moment when Darth tells Luke that he's the boy's father. They all have Vader saying "Luke" *because he did!* It should be clearly heard in our minds, James Earl Jones' voice saying "Luke." It's gone now. When surveyed, very few people can believe it. In this new timeline, it be true. Is there a meaning here? Why *these* changes? Why tarnish the pure gold of the droid? Why no more Luke? Look what they've done to Star Wars and the Light Side. Does the Light Side get equal billing to the Dark? Hell no. We only know of the Dark Side, really. They've killed off the 'Last Jedi' as well as everything good in the world, it seems. Maybe that's why or one reason for the disappearance of "Luke" in Darth's classic line? No more balance to the Force. Darkness won? It seems like an evil, parallel universe has descended upon us and taken us over. Star Wars films, with portrayals of the Dark Side and Light, + and -, are perfect grounds for the Mandela Effect to manifest. *Have your friends, family and almost everything around you moved to the Dark Side?* (I hope I'm wrong and it's just me).

3.   In the film 'Forrest Gump,' there's the famous line, "Life is like a box of chocolates, you never know what you'll get." Or does he say, "Life was like a box of chocolates..."?

❧ To have such a classic film-line as: "Momma always told me, life is like a box of chocolates…" and have it so altered into the past tense, WOW! Even on closed-caption, they write out "was" and it never was 'was.' Why? Is there a meaning here that life used to be made-up of choices? No longer. Maybe we have **no choices** anymore and must accept the new reality forced upon us?

4.   What was the memorable line in the movie: 'Field of Dreams'? Was it, "If you build it, he will come."? Or was it: "If you build it, they will come."?

❧ It's my opinion that if you said to anyone: "If you build it, ___ will come," they'd fill the blank in with "they." Or they should. Who knows? Remember the end of the film? THEY all came from surrounding areas to play ball or watch games on the special field. HE? "They" has been changed to "he." People are not wrong, nor should they be ridiculed for remembering it was "they." Could this also be a message? Are Luciferian filmmakers and secret societies waiting for Satan to come? Are changes to our reality due to dark forces that now manipulate our minds and our physical world from the shadows? I've learned that negatively-charged people tend to *not remember* how it was or see the change, the differences. They are sure this is the way it's always been and we're *nuts*.

5.   In 'The Matrix,' when Morpheus sat down with red and blue pills, do you remember him saying, "What if I told you, Neo, that the world you live in is a lie."?

☯   One more time, you can hear the character's voice express, "What if I told you..." clearly in your head. Check the films, all copies of these films. *Not there anymore.* We're in a universe where it was never said. Yet so many know for certain that it was said. Isn't it very strange that the Mandela Effect tends to demonstrate the artificialness of the world, exactly like the plot of the Matrix? Very fitting that a big M.E. happened in this film. *I wonder what year it actually is and what the real world is like?*

      Also. Near the beginning of 'The Matrix,' when the computer contacts Neo, the first words on the screen are: "The Matrix has you." I've seen the film 20 times, had it on tape and disk. Why do these first words seem not the exact quote? "Has you?"

6.   In the Queen song: 'We are the Champions,' doesn't it end with the lyrics: "We are the champions...of the world."?

☯   It did, now it doesn't. As more people have listened to the band Queen lately because of the movie, some have made a shocking discovery: The song: 'We are the Champions' no longer ends with the words: "...of the world." It's heard on live performances and when other musicians perform the song. But the last line is no longer on any of the original recordings. Listeners are utterly amazed, waiting for last line that does not come. I thought I heard it at the end of the movie (B.R.), but now as I checked online: *it's not in the movie.* Maybe it was there when the film first came out? Not sure. Queen plays the song from 'Live Aid' just before credits roll. It's like the universe has edited it out, as with Vader's line. Does the disappearance of "...of the world" mean: *no more world?* Or the solid Earth you once knew is now gone?

7. In the Beatles song, 'With a Little Help from my Friends,' sung by Ringo, what's the missing word? How does it begin? "What would you __ if I sang out of tune?"

☯ Everyone should remember that the *'correct'* or original version on the recordings had "do." "What would you do..." Joe Cocker sang "do" at Woodstock and so did everyone else when they sang the song in the past. John Belushi and Joe sang 'dueling Cockers' of the song on SNL and it was "do." How could everybody have been wrong? We're not wrong because the recording has been changed to "think." What do you 'think' of that?

8. In the 'Wizard of Oz,' did the Scarecrow ever hold a gun?

☯ Are you kidding me? Scarecrow in the 'Wizard of Oz' with a gun? *Get the hell out.* Here is one of the best Mandelas to show a skeptic who believes it's only mistaken memories. See the film again (free on 123movies.com and ffilms.com). No one remembers Strawman with a gun on the way to Wicked Witch. It was after they saw a sign that read 'I would turn back if I were you.' Where did he get the gun? Who'd give this guy a gun? Why didn't he shoot the Wicked Witch? I'm sure there are no parodies where the straw dude is packin'. But maybe there are now? "What a world, what a world."

9. In the same scene where Scarecrow has a gun, what extra 'weapons' do the Tinman and Lion have?

☯ You don't know? This is a classic film that's been aired year after year on television. How could anyone not know this? The reason is, like other Mandelas, it is a brand new addition. I have not seen one video by any of the Mandela community that points out the anomaly of what other strange things Lion and Tinman also carry. It was searching for Scarecrow's gun that made me examine the film over again...

Only to make a wonderful discovery on my own that no one else had reported, to my knowledge. How could you M.E. people have missed this? Or did these changes suddenly happen? No, it's actually in online photos with the gun: Why do you all not see what is also in the photos? What are the other two carrying? Did you assume Tinman and Lion always had the weapons? They did not. Probably you've seen it, but it just hasn't registered yet because it's unbelievable. The answer, today, is: **Tinman holds a huge Wrench and Lion holds a butterfly net and a big Bug-sprayer!** *What? It's in the online PHOTOS and none of you have talked about it?*

Tinman already carried an ax, but apparently, he needed more armaments as they approached the Witch. He used the Wrench as a club and it was larger than his ax. Cowardly Lion now holds a Bug-sprayer with pump. *My eyes could not believe what they saw.* Dorothy was not armed. (Women are strong in the new world and don't need weapons like the males?). The guys somehow got a hold of weapons. News to me and should be news to a lot of others. The weapons went away after the scene.

10.   When Dorothy and the others first encounter the Wicked Witch, the Witch is on a roof and looks down at them. Before she tossed a fireball at Scarecrow, did she say these words exactly: "Here, Scarecrow! Wanna play ball?" Yes or no?

☯   I initially thought I found a big Mandela here when I first searched for the gun, but I was wrong. Maybe I wasn't? I thought Wicked Witch said to Scarecrow, "How about a little fire, Scarecrow?" at this point and then tossed a fireball at him? When I went over the film again, I found out Witch *did* say the classic line, but it was later, right before she died and lit Scarecrow on fire for a second time. I don't remember Strawman on fire, twice. The earlier line, delivered from the rooftop, doesn't sound familiar to me. "Wanna play ball?" seems odd and even a modern expression. Who knows anymore?

11.   Didn't the Wicked Witch in the 'Wizard of Oz' yell to the weird, flying monkeys, "Fly, my pretties, fly!"?

☯   Margaret Hamilton's distinctive voice once stated the plural: "pretties." It's been imitated thousands of times and is deeply etched into our brains. People weren't wrong. They didn't miss-quote the film. In today's twisted version, Witch merely shouted: "Fly, fly, fly" to the creepy monkeys and repeated it, but never uttered, "pretties." She called Dorothy "my Pretty" a few times, but never used the plural. It's been changed.

12.　Do you remember the flying monkeys in Oz with black hair, red hair or blonde hair?

☯　This has to be another Mandela I found in 'Wizard of Oz' that very few have noticed. I do not remember the flying monkeys having blonde hair or wearing light-colored wigs. Once or twice in the close scenes with Wicked Witch, they do.

13.　Did Glinda, the Good Witch, tell Dorothy to "tap" her heels or "click" her heels?

☯　Why would anyone tap heels? You tap toes or tap feet. When the Cowardly Lion did his song, earlier, he clicked his heels and sang the word "click" when he danced. No one is wrong for remembering that Glinda told Dorothy to "click" her heels "three times." But future generations are left with a slightly corrupted or greatly warped version of what once was. Seems awfully small that she's now told to "tap" heels, but there should never have been any alternation in films, our memories, or anything else. There is also a sudden confusion on whether it was the Good Witch of the North, or was it the East? Wicked Witch of the West, or was it...?

14.　The holographic, big bully Oz, the Great and Powerful, the image of the Wizard amid all the smoke and flames: Was it an eastern mystic with a white turban or was it a big alien-type of head with veins running up it?

☯　Between the smoke, I noticed that it was (now) a big-headed alien without a turban or anything on his head. There were two veins that ran up into the large head. I've seen the film more than 10 times over the years. I would never have guessed alien. I would have said eastern mystic with a thin Fu Manchu mustache. Not sure if others remember the mystic Wizard or was it my imagination? *It was always the alien?*

15.　In 'Snow White,' did the Queen say, "Mirror, mirror, on the wall. Who's the fairest of them all?"? Or did she say, "Magic mirror, on the wall…"?

☯ You guessed it: The evil Queen in 'Snow White' now says: "Magic Mirror." The animated classic begins with a storybook that opens. First thing in the movie is the Queen's line to her mirror written out on first page of the storybook. We now read: "Magic mirror, on the wall…" It was "Mirror, mirror, on the wall…" It's in our memories; it's in every parody; we're not going to forget classic lines in films~ It's a Star Trek title, etc. It's been changed along with all the other Mandela Effects. There certainly is high-tech *Magic* behind the curtain of all the recent transitions on our planet.

16. (My personal favorite) In the Bond film 'Moonraker,' remember Jaws, the big guy with metal teeth? Didn't he fall in love with a blonde girl with glasses and the joke was: When she smiled, she had braces?

☯ The answer was: She had braces. The answer now is: She does not. I remember hating a few of the scenes in 'Moonraker' at the time because it was almost a comedy compared to the first Bond films. Roger Moore said he wanted to add humor when he played Bond. Henchmen Jaws fell in love with a blonde girl, Dolly. She smiled and the gag was she had braces. When I heard the braces weren't there, I immediately watched it again on a free movie channel. GONE! That was the whole purpose of the scene where they met and smiled at each other. I looked close. It was her real teeth without braces. Incredible.

17. What is the correct spelling of the 1989 James Bond film that starred Timothy Dalton? Is it 'License to Kill' or 'Licence to Kill'? Would British film producers actually misspell the title? Do all the old posters, discs and VHS covers have 'License' or (misspelled) 'Licence to Kill' on them? Would the Brits really use bad English in the title of a big, Bond film?

☯ They would in the Dark Universe that has come upon us, not in any real or good world. It's inconceivable they'd do this. Don't they know the English language? It's not a porn flick or from the street, like 'Da Hood.' This is a major motion picture. Could the sinister meaning of 'c,' 'c' be in numerology, which is 33, sacred to the Illuminati? What is more shocking: *Only now* have people noticed the misspelling and called it to the public's attention? Maybe the reason that no one said one word about the error in 30 years is it was always correctly spelled and *only recently has been mystically changed?* Why get anything right in the new, negative universe? Mirror World? Surely, our secret masters believe they have a "licence" to do anything they damn well want to do to us commoners. They believe they have the right to kill us, make wars with us or 'gaslight' us into insanity.

18.   Was Michael Jackson the youngest brother? Or did the pop star have a younger brother than him that was a part of the Jackson 5? Did 6 Jacksons perform onstage as the 'Jackson 5' with Michael *not* the youngest brother? Anyone remember a confusion in the # of Jackson brothers or anyone that ever asked: "Why aren't you called the Jackson 6?"

☯   There is such spookiness with the Jackson Family [besides secret tranny factor] *that it is unbelievable.* Few have noticed a massive Mandela Effect with this odd family. It concerns the question: Who is the youngest of the Jackson brothers? Records say Michael was born in 1958 and Randy, three years later, in 1961. *Hang onto your hat. Randy?* Most people do not remember 6 performing Jackson brothers. They had a 'spare' Jackson they could plug in so the group could perform as J5? No. J5 performed with 6 brothers on many television shows and no one remembers this, hardly. People remember: Jackie, Jermaine, Marlon, Tito and the youngest: Michael. But to many who've followed the band closely for years, *Randy has just now popped into existence!* We are in a world where there are 6 performing Jackson brothers and 6 Village People, when there were only five previously in our Old World.

We are not talking about a judge on a TV show named Randy Jackson, with glasses. This Randy is another one, *a blood brother in the famous Jackson Family.*

View J5 performances on the Tonight Show, Merv Griffin, etc. It is bizarre to have crowds screaming for the Jackson 5, *then have 6 run out onstage.* Little Randy is on congas. There's more to the strangeness: Put 'Mike Douglas Jackson 5' in YT and Mike asks, "Why aren't you called the Jackson 6?" Baby Randy says, "I just joined the band." At the 7-minute mark, Dom Deluise makes a "Beat It" joke in reference to a very young-looking Michael. The band and audience laugh. How could they and how could the joke be made in the first place? That 'Douglas Show' was in 1974...'Thriller' and 'Beat it' did not come out until 1982, *8 years later!*

Collect group photos of the Jackson 5 in Google Images and examine them closely. You will see a paradox. *Is cloning involved* to explain why some photos have Michael as the youngest, while others show Randy is the youngest? Or has a different universe collided with ours and took it over? Every photo hasn't changed to where Randy is the smallest and youngest. It's bizarre to see an older Randy, then view other photos and Micheal towers over little Randy! TV shows and bios (now) confirm that the baby boy was Randy. This was never the case before. Proof of anomalous contradictions and paradoxes are right in front of you. Open your eyes. Of course, skeptics will say, "You're mistaken. Randy was always a member and the youngest brother." Others who know the Jacksons well, remember that there never was a Randy.

19. Do you remember a 6th person in the Village People who was a black man always dressed in a military outfit? Yes or no?

❧ This is hilarious. To me, it's the funniest, Laugh-Out-Loud, example of the Effect. It was 'The Village People,' now it's just 'Village People.' But that's not the funny part. Do you remember a sixth member of the '70's disco boy-band? A second black guy, a Military Man? GI Joe? No? Google VP, hit Images and scroll down through the many pictures. OMG. These are not later photos where they added another person. It's every picture from the very beginning. Even a star on the Walk of Fame with 6? What? I remember the construction worker, the Indian, the tough biker, black highway-patrol guy and, of course, the cowboy. I remember their faces. There were only 5 characters. But now, there's another black guy, always in variations of military dress from green combat fatigues to officer uniforms or in Navy outfits? No way. Where'd he come from? Military guy just popped into being, from my point of view and most others. Once more, people are left in total disagreement. Some may recall the GI Joe named Alex Briley. There's his whole history with the band, which makes a total of six members. To many, he simply appeared one day, the very same with Randy Jackson.

Has anyone checked the Dave Clark 5? I seriously did, there's still 5.

20.   In 'Risky Business,' when young Tom Cruise's character dances, does he have a colored shirt and no sunglasses or does he have a white shirt and sunglasses?

☯   One more movie glitch and it's a big one: Tom Cruise now slides in and dances without sunglasses and without a white shirt. Seriously? He didn't? Of course, he did. But that's not how the original film is anymore. In all parodies of the scene, everyone wears a white top, no bottoms and sunglasses. They're all not wrong. They remember how it was. Today, it's a colored shirt and no glasses. Things are strangely different.

21.   When Sally Field accepted her first Oscar, did she say these exact words: "You like me. Right now! You like me!"?

☯   Those were not the well-known words Sally Field(s) said at the Oscars, but they are now. A large number of people have mimicked her words to the Academy in shows and in movies. None of them have: "Right now!" inserted in the famous lines and eliminated the word "really." Yet, like movies and lyrics and many other things have unnaturally changed, so has this moment. Check it out, "Right now!"

22.   The famous line in the 'Apollo 13' movie: "Houston, we have a problem." Were those the exact words stated in the movie?

☯   It came out that the classic line: "Houston, we have a problem," said by the Tom Hanks character, was heard by many as: "Houston, we've *had* a problem." [past tense, like Hanks said in 'Gump']. Then, possibly, film copies *flipped back* to the original line? People swore the Mandela happened, that they had heard the variation and maybe they had? Did we momentarily see into the parallel world? Sites marked this, but the movie line now is not in the past tense.

The quote from the real astronauts, stated twice, when they first reported the emergency, was: "Houston, we've had a problem."

23.   Is it the Berenstein Bears or is it the Berenstain Bears?

☻   I definitely remember the Berenstein Bears because I had a joke: "I didn't know they were Jewish." I'm sure I wasn't alone when I first saw their books and videotapes in stores, and cartoons on TV long ago. I would never have made the joke if they were spelled BerenSTAIN. Researchers of the Effect have found old VHS tapes and books and sure enough, they read: 'Berenstain.' This is a famous M.E. and well-known to many people. If there is a dark meaning, is it a smear toward Jewish people that smacks of Hitlerism? A stain on society?

24.   Which is correct? Smokey the Bear? Or Smokey Bear?

☻   Ages ago, I also came up with a joke for Smokey the Bear and it was 'the' was his middle name. Not that funny, but it was cute and I would never have made it if his name was always 'Smokey Bear.' Never had a 'the,' huh? Really? I'm stunned. No one could ever tell me that everyone's been mistaken since the 1950s. I'm supposed to believe: *We're all in error and Smokey never had 'the' as a middle name? I guess we've collectively passed on a misconception and that's what most believe?* No! That's not it. I searched YT and found (not a Mandela video) simply a compilation of every 'Only you can prevent forest fires' with Smokey. Twenty minutes long of 30-second or 1-minute commercials from the '50s to the '80s. There was Rocky and Bullwinkle, who brought Smokey on at the end. There was the one of bears starting a fire at your home, so don't you start fires in their home. Even one Rod Serling narrated of a guy who tossed a cigarette butt out his car window and next day read in paper of a terrible fire somebody started. NOWHERE in the first 40 years of Smokey Bear commercials, from cartoons to real people, do they ever say: "Smokey the Bear." *We must all be delusional? Dreaming?* No, we're not. We have good memories. The planet has transitioned: it is different here, here and here. It is what this book is about as well as all sincere Mandela investigators and reporters. We're not wrong; the world is suddenly *"wrong."* [Different].

25. Is it Looney Toons or is it Looney Tunes?

☯   Why would Looney Toons ever be spelled like musical tunes? Music isn't the main thing, it's the cartoons. Adults and kids remember that it had always been spelled like cartoons, with 2 O's, like Toontown or Tiny Toons. Maybe we're all in a cartoon because today, it's 'Tunes'? Warner Brothers is the parent company. Its animation had been under the banner of 'Looney Toons,' but if you view compilation collections of WB cartoons, one after another, from many decades back, all will begin in colored circles with the words: 'Looney Tunes' and not 'Looney Toons.' How strange. Where did the O's go?

26. Is the cereal spelled 'Fruit Loops' or 'Froot Loops'?

☯   We may have discovered where the Looney Toon's O's went? Possibly, onto the box of Fruit Loops, which is now (and always?) been spelled 'Froot.' Many people remember that 'Fruit' was spelled the normal way. Some claim the cereal's name had flip-flopped? In any case, *reality has become Fruit Loops and Looney Toons.*

27. Is it Metro-Goldwyn-Meyer or is it Metro-Goldwyn-Mayer?

☯   I remember MGM as Metro-Goldwyn-Meyer, not like John Mayer. Nope, it *is* like John Mayer today. From black and white to technicolor movies, the lion-logo roars and the MGM movie begins. "Mayer" in the name appears funny to many who remember it differently. Their 'foggy' memories of the past might be correct, no matter what shifts in reality are in front of our eyes in the present. (Was it "Golden" and not "Goldwyn"?).

28. Is it Oscar Meyer or Oscar Mayer hot dogs and meats? Remember the old commercial where the little boy sang: "My bologna has a first name..."? He even sang the letters. Which spelling is right?

☯ "Mayer" has also replaced "Meyer" in Oscar Meyer hot dogs and meats. I played the famous commercial of the kid [see short story] as I checked for the Effect. I couldn't believe it. My mouth dropped: The boy actually sang "A" for Mayer. Unbelievable. Oscar Meyer doesn't exist in this universe and never did. This is not true in many people's experience. We remember.

'Nestles' is another one. Check old commercials. Don't you remember: "N, E, S, T, L, E, S, Nestles makes the very best...chocolate."? Why is it spelled 'Nestle'? Very weird that old commercials, etc., will play the familiar song, with the "s" (not changed) in the audio, but the picture shows no "s" and has been removed.

29. Do you remember Jiffy peanut butter? Or was it always called JIF?

☯ *Believe it or not, we now live in a world where JIFFY peanut butter never existed!* If you distinctly remember it, you're not from this new universe because there's only been JIF in our timeline or present reality. Product changes have been verified by numerous investigators. Companies, apparently, are telling the truth. In nearly every case, the response to tons of M.E. inquirers is: "It's always been that way." But what if employees at the corporate head office, which would contain their complete records, remember how it was? Wouldn't it be strange to have a clear memory of 'Jiffy,' a brand you've loved since childhood, and searched company records yourself, only to find no trace of it? But everything about the product or every bit of the old world did not get wiped out. Jiffy and thousands of other changed products remain intact in **"residue"** or residual, such as receipts, stubs, old ads, etc. There's plenty of evidence for the original names, before the unnatural changes, in countless examples. Residue evidence supports the idea that those who remember the past are not out of their minds. Or wrong.

30. The Monopoly Man with top hat and tails depicted in the classic board game, does he wear a monocle or not?

☯ All bets are off because he used to wear a monocle, but now he does not. The game has been around since 1935. Most everyone had the game or played it at one time. Some grocery stores play a Monopoly game, also, there's Monopoly scratch-offs. The old guy is everywhere now. I found a dusty Monopoly game on my shelf. Sure enough, the monocle, I remember and most others recall, has disappeared. In a Jim Carrey movie, he had a real version of the Monopoly Man and the guy had a monocle. Some say the Pringles man on the potato chip cans has also lost his monocle. *You know what that means? We have to keep a close eye on Mr. Peanut.*

31.   The well-known paint company with the slogan: 'Cover the World with Paint': Is their name Sherman-Williams or is it Sherwin-Williams?

☯   Why is it that I know this product very well, painted houses for a living with the product, know their slogan and the image of an open can that pours paint onto the globe...yet, missed the question? It was 'Sherman.' It was always Sherman, like the General, the tank, and "set the Way-Back Machine, Sherman." I am very good with faces and words. I know if I've seen that face or word before or if I haven't seen it. My eyes never beheld the word 'Sherwin' before in my life. Sorry to inform the disbelievers, but this brand name has oddly morphed...

It brings up a very important point to those who think these are product upgrades and a part of normal changes in design over time. Not NAME changes! If a product has built up a brand over decades, they are not going to change the name, the spelling of the product. And have consumers think the company is *so stupid they forgot how to spell their own product's name*? Change all the letterheads and storefronts for no good reason? No, sir.

32.   How do you spell the famous store's name that has been around since 1902, with nearly 900 locations and 100,000 employees? Is it J.C. Penney or J.C. Penny?

☯   Certainly, you remember? You've seen their large storefronts, you've seen them in malls and you've probably seen their catalogs. Why is it that if a large number of people were polled on how to spell the store's name, maybe a majority would say it was: J.C. Penny? This is not true because most people are stupid and have gotten it wrong over the years. It's true because, believe it or not, almost instantly, 'Penny' changed to 'Penney.' *Shazam!*

33. Is the litter-product called: 'Tidy Cat'? Or plural: 'Tidy Cats'?

☯   This amazes me because I bought a big, plastic container of 'Tidy Cat.' By the time I'd used it up, the label had changed to 'Tidy Cats.' No shit. I asked people in the area and they unanimously remembered the singular, 'Tidy Cat.' I don't think we got it wrong. I contacted the company and sent an email that asked: "Was the name of your company always Tidy Cats?" I'll never receive a response. Mandelaed companies must be inundated with inquires from M.E. people. If I got a reply, it would most likely be: "Always been 'Cats.'"

34. Which is right? 'Sex in the City'? Or is it 'Sex and the City'?

☯   Now it's 'Sex AND the City.' Producers would never make such a needless, useless, unnecessary change in the title of a very successful show. Producers and people involved with the show, from its inception, (now) report: The title was always 'Sex and the City.' Oh, really? Why is it that every time one of the girls won either a Golden Globe or an Emmy, year after year, the title was always said 'wrong' by the presenters? Every time? Every interview? Amazing 'residue' with this one. "The winner is such and such for 'Sex IN the City!'" They all won many times. If it was gotten wrong *once,* they'd be blasted by the critical Media. If it was gotten wrong in backstage interviews and promos, the mistake would have been immediately corrected. There were no corrections over all those years because these records weren't changed and have survived as 'residue.' You can view compilations of Sarah Jessica Parker, Cynthia Nixon and the others who received their awards. All of the awards were for 'Sex in the City.' Been changed recently. When we view clips from certain award shows, we're seeing way back into another/different world from the transformed one that exists today. I heard it stated on a rerun "Office" episode and they said "in."

35. Is the book and film title: 'Interview with a Vampire' or is it 'Interview with the Vampire'?

❧   Similarly, I remember 'Interview with a Vampire.' I went to see it in the theaters at the time. In today's universe, its title has been changed to: 'Interview with *the* Vampire.' Again, interviews with the stars from years ago reveal that the title was '...a Vampire.' David Letterman announced the original title that most everybody is familiar with. Backstage at the Oscars, it was recorded: "...a Vampire," many times (not '...the Vampire'). Would the author of the book know her own title? If there was one person that would get the title right, it would be the author. Again and again in the interview at the Oscars, Anne Rice stated it was: 'Interview with a Vampire.' She wasn't wrong back then. She is now, because the title has been supernaturally changed to 'the.'

36.   In 'Silence of the Lambs,' did the Anthony Hopkins character of Hannibal Lecter ever say, "Hello, Clarice."?

❧   One more cinematic echo has rolled around in our brains, if you've seen the movie. "Hello, Clarice." Check the movie. Now, he only says, "Good Evening, Clarice."

We will cover a number of Mandela Effects that deal with changed products, brand names, packaging designs and many other unnatural anomalies...as well as answering the questions: how, **who**, why and WHEN? The test [glitches in our reality] continues with artwork, grand statues, monuments and geographical changes due to the Mandela...

37.   Da Vinci's 'Mona Lisa' painting, is it emotionless and not smiling or is the girl slightly smiling or smirking?

❧   People have wondered down through the centuries: Is Mona Lisa smiling? The old thought was she was emotionless. But now she seems to smile. Some have noticed the change and have described it as a "smirk." Also, it seems that in the old reality, her identity was a total mystery. But today, we can look up who she was and her backstory. Her name was Lisa Gherardini. She was "pushed into a wedding with wealthy Florentine merchant, Francesco del Giocondo." News to many.

38.   In Da Vinci's famous painting of 'The Last Supper,' with

Jesus and the apostles, was the Holy Grail in the center of the table or not on the table at all?

☯   Many people remember the golden Grail right in the middle of the table, under Jesus. As do I. The disciple to Christ's left in green appears to still be staring at it with his arms wide open, as if amazed by the chalice. That's what I remember. But there is no Holy Grail on the table. A lost, missing Grail...*sounds familiar.*

39. Michelangelo's phenomenal ceiling in the Sistine Chapel was painted between 1508 and 1512. Its central figure is God's creation of Adam. Whose hand is higher? God's or Adam's?

☯   To most everyone's memories, obviously, God's hand would be higher and was angled slightly downward at Adam's hand. (ET's finger on posters mimicked the mural and was angled down). Presently, that is not the case. Surprisingly, it is Adam's hand that is just a bit higher. God no longer points downward but completely horizontal. This fact baffles people who remember the painting a different way. Does the change suggest another dark, negative reality of what's called "trans-humanism," an Illuminati or fascist view of an ascension of man and a lowering of God? But wait...

40. Do you remember seeing, on the Sistine ceiling, an image of God's bare butt? (What?). Ever remember hearing of such a thing? One more time: Did we ever see *God's ass,* a bare butt, painted high overhead on the famous ceiling?

☯   *You think I'm kidding?* Google "God's butt Sistine Chapel." What do your eyes tell you? These are not photo-shopped images made by millennials. This was painted by Michelangelo, *but not the Michelangelo we know!* The incredible painting, featured in the film 'Agony and Ecstasy' [Rex Harrison as pope and Charlton Heston as Michelangelo], yes, had nudity...but God was never known for 'mooning' us. The shock is very few M.E. people know this. Did it just appear? They all seem to know of Adam's raised hand and low hand of God. *Hey! Look 20 feet over there!* How did New York comedians miss this down through the decades? How did Sarah Silverman not critique God's butt? We know the robed portrait of God pointing and the creation of the Sun next to a golden disk. Now, a few feet away, there's the MOON? Over centuries, popes paraded under this image, *really?* Children never pointed and made fun? No disrespect intended, but I cannot be the first one ever to say it looks like God's wearing PJs and there's an open "poop-shoot"? Jokes are endless. What was Michelangelo thinking? Pope allowed this? Each panel of the ceiling is known for a particular Bible story, and the "rear" version of God is no exception. Suddenly in changed Bible (explored later) there appears a reference to support the naked image. In Exodus 33/23, God says: "...And thou shall see my bare parts."

41.　Do you remember Michelangelo's statue of Moses *with horns?*

☯　The sitting sculpture of Moses now has HORNS! What? Anyone remember that being true? Could this be a clear message from the devil or something very evil? *(Skeptics, are you sure nothing's going on?)*. It isn't the one statue of Moses, it's many statues of Moses and even some paintings. So we're supposed to believe Moses *should* be portrayed with horns? In the new world, it seems, *horns* are not regarded as devilish, but as signs of 'holiness' and 'royalty.' After a little research, I arrived at a web-page where someone asked a logical question: "Why would Michelangelo put *horns* on Moses?" The article tried to justify it by saying they were part of a corona, halo or rays of divinity...that broke off. *You can't make this up, folks*. Moses has horns and Hitler now has sympathetic, blue eyes.

42.　In the painting of a heavyset King Henry VIII, does he hold a turkey leg or a purse in his right-hand?

☯　The portrait of Henry VIII is a lost work by Hans Holbein the Younger. It was destroyed by fire in 1698, but is still well-known through its many copies over centuries. It is the most famous painting of any British monarch. The stout King always held a big turkey leg. There are certainly loads of residue evidence for this fact. But there's been a *change*. The turkey leg has morphed into a purse! Yes, a purse. Strange is the fact that the original has been long gone. All the many copies down through the ages have altered, which must utterly stupefy their owners. They probably remember how the paintings used to look. *Shades of Dorian Gray.*

43. 'The Girl with a Pearl Earring' by Vermeer is one of the most famous paintings of all time. Has it changed recently? Look close. Does it appear different to you?

❧ As you'll discover, just about everything has changed a little or a lot. People are not under Mandela delusions or hysteria; they are not making things different when they've always been the same. It is not the Power of Suggestion. Vermeer's lady is now expressive and she never was before. She has larger eyes, there is emotion in her face. Before, she was bland, expressionless, a little like Mona Lisa. Now she evokes emotion. Google the painting and you'll come to a comparison: One shows the image from the Hollywood movie that starred Scarlett Johansson and the other is the actual (changed) painting. Look at the differences. The painting has changed, but not the residue of the PR, theatrical, image that was supposed to exactly duplicate the painting. It was a special moment in the film where they recreated the painting. The actress evokes nothing, eyes smaller, angle of face is different, hair-wrap is different in length, face shadow is off and even the color of the blouse is completely different. Why add a chair? I've seen the film and remember the iconic painting. If Mandela wave had not struck, (I believe) the image of the painting and replicated image for film would match perfectly. If we changed the new painting to match the actress' photo, we probably would have what the original painting looked like.

44. Remember the golden headdress of King Tut, the boy King? What does it have on its forehead, a snake or a snake and a vulture?

❧ There has only ever been a snake or cobra on the forehead of King Tut. A single snake. But not anymore. Museum curators who remember only a snake must be flabbergasted at the new, weird look of Tut. Now there are two things on his forehead: a snake and a vulture. There's probably a great majority of experts who absolutely are certain that the vulture was always there. They would have all the old (changed) photos and records that supported their view that the vulture always stood next to the snake. This could be the case in every single field. People who remember or can see both worlds in collision and others who've only known the changed world and claim: "You're crazy stupid, it's always been that way."

45.   Does the statue 'The Thinker' hold his chin with his hand or hold his forehead?

☯   People claim that 'The Thinker' has his hand on his forehead. There are images of this (Tebow) position in people. No, the statue has always had hand on the chin to most others and myself and in today's reality. 'Thinker Mandela' might not be a Mandela. Maybe researchers, caught in the craze, have rushed-to-judgement on this one? But. Why have so many seen it or recalled it a different way? Maybe they've looked into another world and a large portion of us don't see it? Who knows?

46.   Is the Statue of Liberty on Ellis Island or is it on Liberty Island?

☯   The statue is on Liberty Island, now. European immigrants were known to have arrived in New York on Ellis Island or passed Ellis Island (with statue). Truthfully, I've never heard of Liberty Island until recently. Seen any "Liberty Insurance" commercials with the statue in the background? Many New Yorkers believe that a reality-shift has occurred and Lady Liberty has moved. Liberty Island touches New Jersey. It could be said that the "new location" is no longer in New York harbor, but in New Jersey. The confusion in locations of the statue has never happened before, before the Mandela Effect. Now there's a bridge in NY that few seem to remember.

47.   Has the torch section of the Statue of Liberty been open to the public in the last 100 years?

☯   Tourists have claimed that they have been up in the torch part of the statue and probably have photographs. How can it be possible since the official report is that section has been closed off to the public ever since the Black Tom explosion of 1916? No one remembers this attack by Germans that stopped munitions from being supplied to Allies before U.S. entry into WW1. The massive explosion damaged the skirt and arm of the statue. We remember Pearl Harbor and 9/11, but not this blast that supposedly killed 4, injured hundreds and was felt for many miles around. This event was not a part of our former history.

Neither was U.S. west coast known for being attacked during WW2. Now we discover it was, with the June 21, 1942 bombing of Fort Stevens in Oregon.

48.   In Washington D.C., there is the Lincoln Memorial that we have seen in photos and films hundreds of times. How do you remember the hands? Were they the same and held the front part of the chair? Or was the left-hand different than right and made a fist?

❧   Google and examine photographs of the Lincoln D.C. statue. You'll discover that the hands are different. The left one makes a fist. They were both the same. A 'fist' symbolizes violence, conflict and war. Lincoln was a man of peace who ended the Civil War. He was, in the reality I remember. Why would the artist mutate Lincoln (or Moses)? No one actually removed the old hand and replaced it with another. This was done remotely, 'magically' (scientifically). The inscription written above Lincoln says: "Temple." I'm not sure if that was the right (previous) word that was carved there?

49.   What is on top of the Capitol Building? The famous, white, domed structure we are all familiar with and seen hundreds of times. What do you think is on the very top? Shouldn't this be well-known, common knowledge and certainly never up for debate? Americans should know and also those in the D.C. area. It had to have been viewed in countless movies over many decades. Is it a giant flagpole or something else?

❧   Oh, it be something else. Quite terrifying, in my opinion. It's a 20' bronze statue of a 'warrior woman' called the 'Statue of Freedom' and also '**Armed** Freedom.' They say: "Not to be confused with the Statue of Liberty." The original name for it was "Freedom Triumphant in War and Peace." The statue was designed by artist Thomas Crawford in the mid 19th Century. According to every official record, it has stood there since 1863. *1863!* Are you kidding me? Since the Civil War? Why does no one remember it being there over the last 156 years? This is news to almost everyone. Here is official information about it:

"Her crest peaks at 288 feet above the east front plaza of the U.S. Capitol. She is a female, allegorical figure whose right-hand holds the hilt of a sheathed sword, while a laurel wreath of victory and the Shield of the United States are clasped in her left-hand. Her chiton is secured by a brooch inscribed "U.S." and is partially covered by a heavy, Native American–style fringed blanket thrown over her left shoulder. She faces east towards the main entrance of the building and the rising Sun. She wears a military helmet adorned with stars and an eagle's head which is itself crowned by an umbrella-like crest of feathers. Although not actually called "Columbia", she shares many of her iconic characteristics."

This is horrific to me because women should not be warriors, killers, soldiers. They should not even be 'defenders of freedom' on the front lines of war. Today, they are, in fake wars. They're in modern movies (and commercials) in barbarian battle scenes, and that was never true. The image of female destroyers (outside of good Nemesis, Justice, who wipes out evil and should never have been blindfolded in court) is abominable. But not in the new, dark world descending upon us. Not in a wicked society blasted by Mind Control methods, conditioned for us to do the wrong things, bad behaviors, instead of the right things and good behaviors. Not in a world where every TV commercial, every show, every cartoon and every movie has empowered WOMEN and *emasculated men!* 'Alita, Battle Angel,' 'Wonder Woman' and every portrayal in Media of women, lately, have them so fucking powerful, brilliant, nasty, vicious...while males are stupid, inept, impotent, weak and useless. Have you not noticed this reversal and how upside-down and backwards everything is from what it should be and what it once was, yesterday? [Young dudes grow beards today and shave their heads (backwards) and appear, basically, like galley-slaves. We're all slaves, but we don't have to look like slaves. What happened to hippies, freedom, peace and love, hair, the virility of Samson, good music, good films, good role models, etc.?].

This *new* 'Armed Freedom' statue, with stars and sword and shield, *we're all supposed to believe stood atop the Capitol*

Building for the last 156 years? Don't believe it - yet, you *must* believe it since the records and old movies support its existence. No one placed it there recently. No, it's been there for a century and a half. That is, in the other reality, not the one most all of us know and remember. A male soldier should have been the symbol long ago during the age of chauvinism. The very idea that there's another female besides Lady Liberty and Columbia? And she suddenly appeared to many? Astonishing. I guess it's not so strange that the statue is perfectly in line with the New Order of *females rule, and males follow.*

I remember a big flagpole on top of the Capitol Building.

50. Do you remember the giant, carved images of presidents at Mt. Rushmore in South Dakota to be just heads? Or do you remember Washington had a collar and partial jacket?

☯ Mandela investigators have noticed that the faces of the presidents seem to be looking in *different directions* than what they were before. The most stunning difference is people remember unfinished figures that were only heads. But now, George has a ponytail and wears a jacket with a detailed collar? Lincoln is shown with the top part of his hands that clutch books. I sure don't recall the jacket, hand and books. Mistaken memories? Or a change of reality where the figures were a little more completed? ("We're not in Kansas anymore.").

51. Can you name any of the top 10 tallest statues on Earth, much taller than Christ the Redeemer or the Statue of Liberty? Not even one?

☯ Why should you be able to name them or even know what they look like? To most people, *they've just arrived on Earth.* Pop! Google 'tallest statues' and you'll be amazed and maybe frightened? Where the heck did these giants come from? Why aren't they common knowledge? Here is a list of the 10th highest to the very tallest:

10. Grand Buddha, Lingshan, China, 88 meters.
9. Great Buddha, Thailand, 92 meters.
8. Peter the Great, Russia, 96 meters.

7. Sendai Daikannon, Japan, 100 meters.
6. Emperors Yan and Huang, China, 106 meters.
5. Guan Yin of the South Sea of Sanya, China, 108 meters.

This beautiful, white tower of a 3-faced goddess that looks out to sea is absolutely extraordinary, as are the others on the list. She's called the "Goddess of Compassion."

4. Ushiku Daibutsu, Japan, 110 meters. An all-bronze statue.
3. Laykyun Setkyar, Myanmar, 116 meters.
2. Spring Temple Buddha, China, 153 meters.

It took 11 years to build and was made of 1100 copper cast pieces.

1. Statue of Unity, India, 182 meters!

This incredible statue honors Indian leader Sardar Vallabhbhai Patel, called the "Iron man of India." [Who?] It's located near Vadodara and was built across the Sardar Sarovar dam. Six hundred feet tall makes it the height of two football fields stacked on top of each other. Seriously? I never heard of the guy. Why not Mahatma Gandhi?

There is, of course, a full history on the construction of each of these grand giants that dwarf people to almost the size of ants. Again, these wonders are *news* to a lot of us. Shouldn't we have heard of them before or, at least, know what they look like?

More strange and amazing structures and statues seemed to have *suddenly appeared.* Here are new additions to the colossal giants or fantastic buildings, very few people remember or have ever seen before. You be the judge. Look them up and see if they are new to your eyes? The oddities will, again, astound you. Where have they been?

- Bubanj Memorial, Serbia.
- Buzludzha UFO Building, Bulgaria.
- Christ of the Ozarks, Arkansas.
- Guanyin of Nanshan, China.
- Mekedonium, Somenik, Macedonia.
- Our Lady of the Rockies, Montana.
- The Mother Calls, Volgograd, Russia.
- War Memorial, Montenegro.
- Podgaric Monument, Croatia.
- Stone Flower, Croatia.

52. Does this sound familiar or strange to you? A gigantic Buddhist temple in Thailand in the shape of an orange *flying saucer* with a big Buddha and 300,000 smaller, golden statues of Buddha around the temple? Heard of it?

☯ We are well aware of the Taj Mahal, Angkor Wat and other holy places on the planet. But who's really heard of Wat Phra Dhammakaya in Thailand whose shape and dimensions are so unique? The "Flying Saucer" temple has been around for *50 years!* Why only in the last few years (or months) has anyone heard or known of it? Could it have, yes, *suddenly appeared,* along with other mysterious statues and changes and histories? Now you can find it was started by the meditation teacher Luang Pu Sodh Candasaro in the early 20th Century. "It aims to adapt its traditional Buddhist values in modern society. It deploys modern technology, marketing methods..."

There are photographs of what appears as a million Buddha followers, clad in orange robes, worshiping at the feet of the golden Buddhas or in front of the *spaceship!* The disk-shaped, orange-lit temple, has a central dome. At it's four entrances is a colossal red flag with the silhouette of a flying saucer. The building is also called the "Dhammakaya Cetiya,' and is a symbol of "world peace through inner peace." The fantastic temple covers nearly a thousand acres! Wow. The complex contains more than 150 surrounding buildings. Some have claimed it as the "Largest Temple in the World." Strange, and surely not familiar to most people, even world travelers and students. *For fifty years,* UFO Buddhist Temple is not something everyone would have missed or overlooked. But apparently, they have.

53. How many Great Walls are there on Earth? One? Two? Three? More?

☯ There was only one Great Wall on Earth, before: the Great Wall of China. Now there are other "Great Walls." Mandela researchers have pointed to unbelievable land changes that will be examined later in some detail. With the "shrinking" of the size of China, people have noticed and reported vast changes to China's Great Wall. (Mongolia was a small country, now it's huge, and

China is about the size of the U.S.)?

Today, in our transmogrified world that more and more people are opening their eyes to, we can read about the...

* Great Wall of India.
* Great Wall of Pakistan.
* Great Wall of Peru.

These are fabulous structures that are, oddly, not in people's memories. Look them up and study their backstories and information. Do you see a pattern here?

One of the most fascinating aspects of the Mandela Effect is the possibility that new ancient ruins on land and under the sea, have suddenly appeared, crystallized into being, recently. Investigate. Some really have. These sites are new to many people, while others will contend: "No, they were always a part of our history."

This concept of new things that have 'magically' moved or manifested from a parallel universe, like islands that have appeared and islands that have disappeared...

If true, then *what have we lost?* What ruins do we distinctly remember, but no longer exist on the planet anymore. Worth investigating.

54. Take a good hard look at the Moon. Carefully examine photos of the full Moon in Google Images. Study the disk closely. If you remember what the Moon looks like or looked like, can you tell? Has there been a change in our satellite's appearance? Does the Moon look different to your memory? Or is it the old 'Man in the Moon' we have known all our lives?

☯   *There's been a freaking CHANGE!* Found minutes ago, as I penned these words for my M.E. book. Here was where I wanted to insert what researchers have found about Luna in regard to Mandela. Others have reported, the Moon appears:

Brighter, closer, clearer, sharper, in "HD," at different angles as it turns in the sky. The points on the crescent Moon look odd. Now, most or all of that could be true, but there's something more important y'all are missing: There really is **no 'Man in the Moon' anymore**. Mare Imbrium and the seas to the east composed the eyes of the "man." There's been a radical *shift*.

I fucking know the Moon! The few readers of my novels know I have stories that mention one lovely crater in particular: **Arzachel**. Sounds like "archangel," doesn't it? ('Son of Zog,' 2nd novel of the 'Traylogy'). It's a beautiful crater, extremely unique, with a distinctive high peak and a single large crater on the floor of the bigger crater. No other lunar crater goes up and down like that in the center. I have collected pictures of Arzachel since High School! That was a long time ago. I've had a Rand McNally's Map of the Moon on my walls in college. *The crater called to me,* for some reason? Do you know how many libraries have holes in their old astronomy books in western Pennsylvania because of me? Why was I drawn to this one specific place in dreams and stories? Home? I wish. Arzachel has warm snow and rains of different colors. In my dreams, anyway. Ah. *Don't you think I know where on the Moon my base is located...or was located?* It's not where it was! I only discovered this, NOW. Wow.

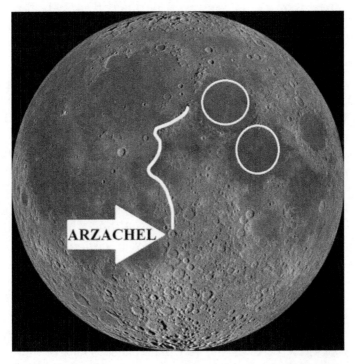

I've studied the Moon for decades, even called it "Home." It's shifted down and to the left. See Arzachel. It was a jewel around the Lady of the Moon's neck. (Will explain) Arzachel was located in the exact center of the Moon. And I should bloody well know! Does that look like the very middle of the Moon? It is still among the cluster of craters that should be around it, but it's maybe *500 miles southwest* of where it should be or was. *Doh!*

To see the Lady, who is in profile, better: The white line up from the crater traces a neck, chin, mouth, eyes and forehead. What's been called "mouse ears" make up the hair of the Lady in two parts. She was never full front and directly in the center of our satellite. She was up and to the right more, which pulls her "Arzachel" neck pendant up to the center of the disk.

The circles are the Sea of Tranquility and the Sea of Serenity. The distinctive, oval Sea of Crisis (easily seen from Earth), to the right of Tranquility, was closer to the edge. Tycho also seems too far left. Copernicus is too low. Everything appears pulled to the left and down. I didn't expect to get *rocked* when I checked the new Moon. Not the New Moon, but a transformed one. Don't get me wrong, the Moon could very well be real or as real as anything else. But it's a different Luna that contains the remains of another timeline and a different history than the one that was.

Today. We'll see old movies or drawings or images of the Moon and it appears that it has always been this way: shifted down and to the left. No, it hasn't. In the Lost World of the past, the image of the Moon was different, there was a "man" in the center.

Has there been a repeating pattern where *men have been eliminated and women have been empowered?* It's interesting (it seems) that it's no longer a man's world. The new world is a woman's world, with Woman Warriors, and the men are barefoot, in the kitchen with the baby. The 'woman soldier' suddenly on top of the Capitol Building? Women on front lines of war, strong and powerful, is the new trend in every movie, commercial, etc. Here we have the Lady of the Moon thrust to the forefront and center stage.

55. Take a good hard look at the planet Mars. Really examine the statistics in the present reality. Does today's Mars coincide with the Mars you knew or does the red planet also seem different from your memory?

☯ Mars is smaller. Before, Mars was considerably larger in size.

It wasn't as large as Venus, but it wasn't much smaller, as it is now. The length of the Martian day was and is very similar to Earth's day of around 24 hours. In the Old World, I concluded WHY someone would weigh a little less on Mars than they would on Earth. This was because it is farther from the Sun than Earth and it is in a longer/slower orbit. Weight is a result of movement, not mass or size of a planet. Go up in an elevator and you gain weight. Go down in an elevator and you lose weight. My "brilliant" conclusion, I was so proud of, answered the question. *You must consider all movements.* If our day or rotation around our axis was the same as the Mars' rotation, then our weight on Mars would be the same – and it wasn't. It was a little less. Mars, in a slower orbit, was why we weighed slightly less. But that was then and this is now. Guess what, friends? All that can be tossed out the window! Today. Little, biddy *Mars has hardly any gravity at all!* What?

(How many times must we scratch our head, and question what was once common knowledge? This is because of the Mandela).

It's unbelievable to people who remember how it was. I'm supposed to believe today's official statistics, what every record now reports? When you look up Mars in this reality, you will discover that:

If you weighed 100 pounds on Earth, you'd way only 38 pounds on Mars! Excuse me. *Naw!* Nothing makes sense anymore because the **Martian day is still the same as the Earth day**. It's still the 4th planet and has not gone beyond Pluto in an extremely slow orbit around the Sun. So why the heck do you weigh, and always have weighed, only a third of your weight on Mars, similar to the Moon? No frikkin' way. Those were not the "rules of the Solar System" or even remotely how physics work. No one on Mars, in the past or in the present, should only weigh about a third of their weight on Earth. But everything today tells us that they do. *It's just wrong.*

We have to question everything now and we never had to before. It's so easy and lazy and stupid to conclude: People simply remember differently from the way it is and always was. *No, mam!* People who remember how it was or the Old World have good memories. They will not align themselves with the dark Shadow World that has only recently been set upon us, where everything is a little different. It's also possessed a lot of human beings and thrust them to the Dark Side. Why don't they remember how it was anymore? Things are now *negatively-charged.*

Let's examine the amazing "Egypt of Mars" on the Cydonia Plain. [My third book in the Traylogy: 'The Cydonian War']. Centrally located on the planet are unnatural anomalies, massive structures, that dwarf the colossal constructions of Egypt. These "buildings" are on the order of what Atlantis created, before the continent sunk. The famous, much criticized, "face" is truly a representation of a face and not natural or "trick of the light." It is a structure with steps, pathways, railings and an interior that stretches **the length of one mile!** In my opinion, it has always served the same purpose as the Sphinx at Giza. Could be an enormous, electrical, ground-contact point for the Great Pyramid Energy-Broadcaster or Power Beacon. It is along these lines that the structures were made: a scientific purpose. Sphinx seems to work in concert with the main pyramid and taps or stabilizes the natural EM energies, no matter what planet you were on. Face on Mars and a (Sphinx) Face at Giza.

[Three pyramids in the City correspond in pattern or layout to the 3 at Giza and also Orion's belt stars. It's been known for a long time that Giza's main pyramids match Orion's belt stars, but do they today? The brightest star was always the center one and matched the brightest, biggest pyramid, the Great Pyramid, which used to be in the middle. (It's magically moved near Cairo now). When I looked up the present magnitude of the belt stars, I found out they had not switched. It would be interesting either way: If center and brightest star, Alnilam, had also moved to the one on the end, or did not? Alnilam remained the brightest and right in the center of the three stars. The uncomfortable truth is the main pyramids at Giza still corresponded in their positions, but no longer matched Orion's brightness or magnitude, as they did].

I've studied the Martian Cydonia area since the 1970s. Here's the problem, as I examined the location in today's reality:

Where's the obvious Big Pyramid or largest pyramid on Mars? There was no question what pyramid was the Great Pyramid of Mars? It was always the one across from the Face (west) and in the complex called "The City." It was five-sided as others on the planet appear to be. But now, there's the "D&M Pyramid," south of the City and it is absolutely huge. Seems very different to me. I remember the name and that pyramid was always at Cydonia, only smaller, not as tilted. Now, D&M Pyramid could be viewed as the Great Pyramid on Mars. Confusion in this area wouldn't have happened before M.E.

56.   How many ringed planets are there? One? Two? Three? More?

☯   I am a good theoretical physicist. I've loved astronomy since I was a kid and aced a college course. I've owned a few telescopes and a beautiful Celestron at one time. I've seen 4 comets, including Halley's. I was fortunate enough to view Mercury one clear night; Copernicus and Galileo never did that. Take it from me: Uranus and Neptune have always had rings. They were very faint, but they've been known about for decades. No Mandela. The ring around Jupiter seems new to me. That could be a M.E.? Also, one word about we were once in the Sagittarius arm of the galaxy and now we're in the Orion Spur? Who'd you hear that from? DeGrasse Tyson, Bill Nye, Kaku? Those guys are TV actors and their bios will tell you they are actors.

If we suddenly shifted our position light-years in space, many/many close stars would also change position to our view and we'd see different constellations in the night's sky. It's basically the same constellations. But. *We may have exchanged places with a Mirror World* that was located there and a whole new parallel history for mankind, galactically. We may not have moved positions in space. We may have switched worlds, switched polarities, switched with a different history, one that originated in the Orion Spur? Maybe? Merged with our negative/anti-matter counterparts that settled in a different part of the Milky Way? From there, the parallel, our night's sky is what it is today (like the other?).

If you followed that train of thought: I'm saying the stars are in slightly different positions. If we, now, took a spaceship [pretend we can] back to exactly where we were in the Sagittarius arm, the stars would not be arranged in familiar constellations we know. They'd appear jumbled. Just a theory. If it's a new Earth, is it a new galaxy?

57.   Which large Egyptian pyramid at Giza was in the center, among the three, and aligned with the Great Sphinx? Is it the second largest, called Khefren, with inferior inner chambers? Or is it the largest one called the Great Pyramid with high, inner chambers? A simple question: Which pyramid was always in the middle?

☙   Not so simple a question because **THE GIZA PYRAMIDS HAVE SWITCHED POSITIONS!** Besides cosmic changes, you wouldn't think the great 'monuments' on Earth have changed, now, would you? Moses' horns, Lincoln's fist, Mt. Rushmore and many more. How about one of the biggest impossibilities or contradictions or clashes of worlds, whatever you want to call it:

Bottom line: *Great Pyramid was always the one lined up with the Great Sphinx in the middle of Giza.* No more. *Now Khefren is in the center and Great Pyramid is the one on the end!* It is inconceivable, but absolutely true. No one physically moved them. We are now definitely inside a world with a completely different ancient history.

When I first saw Mandela vids that mentioned the GP, initially, they mentioned a new entrance on the Great Pyramid. I thought: *No way.* It's nearly 500 feet high and sits on a gigantic square of enormous monoliths. There's no entrance along the ground of the large square. I saw a photo online that looked like forced-perspective; the foreground picture was not attached to the background pyramid. I continued and searched for something/anything that could have been altered at Giza. This was *after* I searched other monuments and was convinced: There could be some very big or small changes in everything and we have to really open our eyes to truly see what's in front of us.

At first, I didn't quite get what the Mandela community stated: that the Great Pyramid seemed to be much closer to the city of Cairo. That was in the back of my mind as I stared for an anomaly in beautiful colored photos of all three pyramids and spectacular skies. Suddenly. A fuckin' 'ton of bricks' smashed me once my eyes cleared and I actually realized what I was seeing! *What the fuck was Khefren doing in the center?* OMG. OMG! OMG!! It was never this configuration before. How long did I view these pics and not see? Now I know why Great Pyramid seemed so close to the city. *Because it is now and never was before! Wowie.*

Sphinx remains in perfect alignment with the middle pyramid, but that pyramid is no longer the Great one. Why would an inferior pyramid be in alignment with the Sphinx? [In my story 'Lightmare,' the question is answered with an alternate history where Sphinx dates to the time of Khefren. Not in my reality].

Remember. There were never mummies or a sarcophagus found in large pyramids. They are not tombs, but Tesla-based power stations in a world grid of magnetic energy. The coffer resembles a bathtub and supports legends of initiates being zapped with such powerful, electro-magnetic forces that they left the pyramid super enlightened~

Now we read that there's a coffer in the Khefren pyramid? This has to shock Egyptologists that remember how it used to be: only one coffer. *A second coffer at Giza, other than the King's chamber in the GP? And a "black coffer" at that?* No freaking way! A "Son's Chamber" in Khefren, like GP has (misnamed) King and Queen's Chamber? *Son?* Then to discover that Khefren has some above-ground passages when it never did before? Incredible.

There are many photographs of the Great Sphinx, head on, as the Sun rises and strikes the face, directly. Behind it was always the Great Pyramid. *Now it's Khefren.* The "Second Pyramid" is the most easily recognized from a distance. It looks like it has a large 'nipple' on top, which are really outer, casing stones. It seems tallest in some group shots and that's because it's on higher ground than the GP, now on the end. The idea that you have to walk up a small hill from GP to the higher-elevated Khefren in middle is completely new to me and others. I was taught that the entire Giza plateau was a virtual, engineering impossibility, in that they shouldn't have had the means to perfectly level/flatten such a huge area, let alone place stone wonders upon it. Now, it's *not level* and you walk up a hill to the center pyramid? Very, very strange.

Other Mandela info showed a rectangular section under the Sphinx's ear, not there before or previously known. A "void" in the GP, possibly new chambers and "stairs"? That's different. What is not a Mandela is people saying: "One or more of the pyramids had capstones. I remember it went up to a point." Nope, and that makes no sense. The power stations are many thousands of years old, worn, beaten, stripped, and the gold conductor or quartz crystal capstones have been removed a very long time ago.

A personal note that happened only a week back: The Giza revelation was a "game-changer," as they say, a real mind-blower for me. I've lectured on Atlantis, the ancient world grid, was on 'Coast2Coast with George Noory.' You can view my interviews on YT and hear my radio shows on the subject of Tesla energy and ancient pyramids. So I ran to my webmaster of ancient mysteries with this news: he'd supported me in the past, posted my articles for more than a dozen years. Pyramids are all over his site. He's a mathematician. He's posted many various pages of theoretical speculation of other worlds, parallel realities, possibilities, etc. But. We've had our problems recently [Is it just me, or has everyone gone to the Dark Side, lately?]. He absolutely didn't see that the pyramids switched and he should have. I am not wrong, but also not in the majority. THANK THE STARS others saw my point of view too, and remembered GP was always in middle. It felt so good to know I wasn't alone, especially after a big fight with the webmaster. I knew it was a relative argument and no one was right or wrong. But he demanded he was right and I was a lunatic, 100% wrong and Khefren was always in the middle. He suggested I had Alzheimer's. *That hurt.* Later, I realized this guy called every Mandela person foggy in the head and insisted nothing could unnaturally change and it was always the way it is now. He could easily explain the M.E. anomalies and that was *without doing any research into them. Without looking.* How arrogant, prejudice and unscientific. Wow. Nothing could convince him. Not even the fact that the King James Bible has unnaturally changed. (This will be explored in depth later in this book).

I went through my extensive library of paperbacks and hardbound books on Egypt and the pyramids. Everything, in this reality, supports the webmaster. I pulled out my hardbound copy of Peter Thompkins' book called 'Secrets of the Great Pyramid' and studied it. The book is laced with wonderful, intricate drawings, pencil and ink, as well as an array of old photos. The book is 50 years old and a great source of information. I couldn't help but laugh at the exquisite artwork of the pyramids. Every one had Khefren perfectly centered and in alignment with the Sphinx. Of course, the far superior Great Pyramid was positioned off to the side.

Never, never, never would anyone have confused one Giza pyramid with another. But now, after the Mandela-wave/change, it seems our memory, polarity, history and old universe have switched. Now there's confusion in every field.

Did my former friend, the webmaster, (who'd changed personality, it seemed) not see the way it was before Mandela because he'd joined the masses and already went Dark Side? [Don't get body-snatched, *stay awake!*].

58.   Have land masses and whole continents changed shape? Overnight? Have countries really changed their borders in a flash? Does the globe appear different to you? Or is it just our imaginations? Check maps yourself and decide...

❧   Is South America where you remember it in relation to North America? What's wrong with this picture? Get a map of the globe and LOOK! See where it is today? Well, it wasn't in that position years ago. *Central America and South America have now been 'magically' stretched more than 1000 miles east, into the Atlantic Ocean!* There were no tidal waves. "Big Pond" has drastically shrunk; South America is much closer to Africa. Pacific Ocean takes up almost an entire hemisphere and it never did before.

Do a test: Google "hand-drawn world maps" and see what turns up? You'll be shocked, those who think South America was always way east and fairly close to Africa. In blind drawings where people have attempted tracing the continents from memory, why do they consistently put SA directly under NA? One after another, maybe 9 times out of 10, the outline is drawn 1000 miles west of where it is on maps today. Why don't we remember South America more east or much further south? Countless people recall it far west from where it is, as demonstrated in memory-drawings.

59.   Does the Panama Canal run east and west or more north and south? Does the country of Panama run east and west or more north and south?

❧   These are very easy geography questions. Shouldn't everyone know the simple answers? Yesterday, the answer was: Panama was a vertical country and the canal went east and west. Today, the land's been *unnaturally pushed* far east (with addition of Costa Rica) so Panama is now a horizontal country and the canal runs more north and south. Just look, use your eyes and memories. Why would anyone think So. America was directly under the U.S. since old maps and every map (almost) now shows that it's *not even under Mexico and barely under Florida?* Old, black and white, 'Universal International' films began with the turning globe and there's lower America way east from upper America. Millions of us shouldn't distinctly remember a more west South America. But we do. This prime Mandela does not result from a lot of idiots being unaware of basic geography. It comes from the fact that land masses are very different...in the new world.

60. Is Costa Rica an island in the Caribbean or is it not an island and part of the mainland and borders Panama?

☯   Are you really going to answer: "It was always on the mainland and borders Panama"? I guess, most will? Because, this is *not* how many remember it. They recall: 'Costa Rica Island.' It slips off your tongue: "Costa Rica Island." The "island nation of Costa Rica." It was located in the Caribbean, southeast of Mexico and southwest of the Cayman Islands. Now, it is part of the mainland. People remember Nicaragua bordered Panama. But today, *mainland Costa Rica is in the way?*
    (I conducted a small survey here in LA among Spanish people. Some remembered 'the island of Costa Rica.' Some remembered it was connected to Panama. Amazing. Try the experiment yourself: Find a person who knows Costa Rica, been there or find someone who is native to Costa Rica. Ask if they were born on an island or not? Some might say *yes* and some might say *no.* There should not be any confusion in this area. Want to bet? There is now).

61. Wasn't the Rock of Gibraltar a strategic island [WW2] inside the mouth of the Mediterranean? Or has it always been a part of the mainland?

☯   Why do numerous people remember the "Rock" was an island? Possibly, because *it was an island,* in the old reality? It was once out in the sea between Spain and Morocco. I thought it was an island that looked like El Capitan. No, Gibraltar is a mountain range, connected to the mainland. (See residue evidence later in book of the island of Gibraltar and the island of Costa Rica).

62.   Which country is more south? Australia or New Zealand? Also, is New Zealand a single strip of land or composed of two islands?

☯   In (Columbus') New World, the "land down under" should now be New Zealand. It's moved from northeast of Australia to southeast. Surprise. NZ was always a single piece of land. No more. Now there exists a "North Island" and a "South Island" divided by Cook Strait? I guess, for ages, there have been *two islands?* Below, the 'Antarctic Ocean' no longer exists and has been changed into the "Southern Ocean," most are not familiar with.

Australia appears smaller to many people and too close to northern islands. It was more south and far out into the ocean. What's the capital of Australia? Shouldn't we automatically know the continent's capital? I thought it was either Sydney or Melbourne? Wrong, again. It's Canberra! Since when?

63.   Here's the easiest geography question: Which country is larger (square miles) in size, the United States or China?

☯   Actually it is a difficult question, in this reality. It was never a question before: China was bigger. *China was much bigger!* Today, if you count Alaska, America is larger. If you count all disputed territories of China, China is larger. Why do most people remember China being a massive country? They're not wrong. Do memories persist because borders really have altered instantly and only a relative few see the paradox?

64.   Is Mongolia a large country at the present time or was it an ancient empire from long ago?

☯   Old World answer may be a third option: Most people recall Mongolia being a small country below Russia. Now check Mongolia on a map and it is *unbelievable.* Huge! It takes up most of northern China, where before was all-China. Yes, Great Wall has also changed to a shorter length. There was a long border between Russia and China. It's gone, presently, and they only border each other a little at the far east end. This is because enormous Mongolia has taken over the landscape, which is not in our memories, mostly. Were there ever Mongolians at the Olympics? (I'm sure there exists a history of Mongols at Olympics). There will be from now on. Quite a few people polled believed the country was a fabled land from long ago. Also. Tibet was a province of China, but now it's a separate country and has helped shrink the size of China.

[Personal note: I have never seen or ever remember seeing a Mongolian contestant on a TV show before in more than 60 years of watching TV. Last night, for the first time, I did. Next, they'll be Huns or the Ottoman Empire? I just checked "Ottoman Empire." Records say: it ruled parts of Europe, Asia and Africa up to the 20th Century. How can that be true?].

65.   Examine a world map or globe and view Canada and Alaska. Do they appear the right size from what you remember?

❧   Canada has been "decimated" by water! There's too much ocean now, huge lakes and new lakes. Canadians do not remember the "Great Bear Lake," but there it is. Southampton Island is a huge island at the mouth of the Hudson Bay. Why do many Canadians not remember it? I remember Canada's area being a lot bigger than the 48 states. Not so true anymore. Water has taken away much of the land. (When the transition happened, it happened quickly. We turned around or woke up one morning and our world was different).

Look at the size of Alaska. *It has morphed to at least 2 times larger than what it was.* Now it is more than 2/3s the size of the U.S. Alaska's west coast is different: irregular, like a 3-fingered glove. America was hundreds of miles from Russia across the Bering Strait. Now we're only "55 miles" away? Alaska nearly has a curved land-bridge that extends to Russia? Eastern U.S.S.R. looks too thin. Below the Bering Strait is a (new) Russian island called 'Savoonga.'? *(Is this Earth II? Where are we?).*

66. Does the Mediterranean Sea appear different to you?

❧   The opening of the sea seems much smaller, like a little channel. And the entire Mediterranean appears considerably smaller in size. Italy's 'boot' is pulled back a bit like it's about to kick. It has a higher heel. Researchers have noted how close Sicily and Italy are now. The 'boot' almost loses its shape with a semi-attached Sicily. Corsica and Sardinia are different to me. Cypress was just south of Greece. Now, the island is far to the east in the Mediterranean.

67.   Does England angle this way: "/," parallel to Spain, France and Germany? Or, does England angle this way: "\," in an opposed angle to the European mainland?

❧   The country was parallel, but you'll find that England is now at this angle: "\."

68.   Is the United States more south than Hawaii? Or is Hawaii more south than the U.S.?

❧   Wouldn't you think America was south of the Hawaiian Islands? No. Hawaii is below the Tropic of Cancer, below the Baja peninsula and across from southern tip of Cuba and Haiti in the Caribbean. Hawaii is too close to the States. It was way north and much farther out into the Pacific Ocean.

Rather than asking more geography questions on global changes, the following comes from random Mandela people, in their home countries, who know their areas well and have provided videos of the physical changes...

I'll go first with memories of how American states have changed:

California was larger and dominated the west coast, now Oregon and Washington states have grown in size. Baja peninsula appears much longer. South Carolina was larger. Minnesota never had a small spit of land on its northern border that went up. Never. Since when is Michigan in two sections? What? Another half of it continues on the other side of Lake Michigan? Wisconsin stretched more north. *But now, that land belongs to Michigan?* Two Michigans? I'll be darned. That is not the shape of the State of

Maryland! What is Maryland's new territory to the west, almost separated from the other part? NY state was not flat on top, but it is today. Kentucky and Tennessee are in different shapes from what I remember. Ohio was never as large as Pennsylvania. West Virginia is huge and nearly the size of PA. I've gone from hometown Pittsburgh, west, into Ohio a few times and I've never known W. VA. being in the way! It was never there before. If you went west from anywhere in PA., you never ran into West Virginia; it was all Ohio. Now you do. WV once stood totally south of PA. *"This is not America."*

Northern Norway is too thin and is in an unfamiliar shape. The most northern town in Norway was once the "most northern town on Earth." Suddenly. Islands have appeared far to the north of Norway that belong to Norway. Now these (new) islands called "Svalbard" contain the "most northern town" on the planet.

Finland appears an odd shape to many Scandinavians. Sweden is monstrously huge.

Switzerland was located much farther to the northeast, near mountainous, snowy regions. Today, it is west of Austria, south of Germany, directly east of France and right above Italy?

Europe has shrunk, tremendously. Germany is very small and was in eastern Europe, now it's in western Europe. East and West Germany were separated by a wall in the middle. The countries are nowhere near half and half, today. East Germany is much smaller in a section of the northeast?

Ukraine is the largest European country? And Turkey is *enormous,* like a big turkey leg, even larger than the Ukraine. Turkey can just fit in the Mediterranean Sea below Italy's 'boot.' Kazakhstan is more than half the size of China?

Poland is larger than what it was before.

India had a point on its western border. Now that area has been taken by Pakistan.

North and South Korea are *crazy* because the countries were once located near Laos and Vietnam. In the present situation, they are far north and border on Russia? If I asked: What country is in-between China and Japan? Would you be surprised to discover it was Korea? South Korea is strangely bordered by water?

Japan was a straight-shaped country. Now there is a curve in it that was not there before.

The Philippines is located too close to China and Vietnam. This was where Korea used to be.

Africa appears smaller and pushed north toward a smaller Mediterranean Sea and a smaller Europe. Remember that Africa's southern tip was only a bit more north than the tip of South America? Check it today and you'll see a humongous difference; Africa is much more north. Algeria is the largest African country? Northwest or top part of Africa seems "added" in numerous memories. Madagascar was more south, closer to mainland and right across from South Africa. Not now.

What are the countries south of Morocco? To some people these countries have only recently *popped* into existence: Mauritania? (I thought it was an old luxury liner?). And 'Western Sahara.' Who's heard of Western Sahara as a country?

Iran and Iraq have *flip-flopped!* Iran was the one most west. Now, Iran is the one most east.

Haiti and the Dominican Republic have also *flip-flopped.* On the island composed of two countries, Haiti was on the east coast. Now it's the Dominican Republic on the east coast and Haiti is on the west coast. (My surveys have confirmed this).

Puerto Rico was never next to the Dominican Republic; it was more south.

The Bahamas was smaller, further out into the Atlantic Ocean and never so close to Florida. (A Bahamian girl I know confirmed this fact; she was sure Nassau was much farther away from Miami).

Mexico appears thinner, "skinny."

Cuba seems bigger than it was before and closer to the U.S. It blocks or cuts off the Gulf of Mexico.

Ecuador and Peru were nearly the same size. Today, Ecuador has shrunk and Peru has enlarged many times.

Of course, what happened to the lands to the north, around the North Pole? What happened to the ice around the North Pole? Huge, ice cap? It was known to be there. It is nowhere to be seen on Google Earth, or anywhere else, apparently.

We will switch gears to the human body...

69. Are you aware your body is completely different than it was

previously?

❧   The human body as well as our environment has shifted to something *different.* Look up the evidence. Learn about your new bodies:

There is bone behind the eye sockets and it was never there before. Here was one of the first Mandela Effects that I found online (still skeptical, later I was convinced) and I did not know what to think. Yes. Plenty of old, creepy, horror movies had snakes that went in and out of eye sockets. If not real skulls, they were representations of real skulls and there was no bone that blocked them. Today, every skull has only two, small, concave areas behind the eyes. Ping-Pong balls can barely fit in the sockets. Yet, nurses have been filmed and they definitely stated this bone of "protection" was not there before. They reported: You could stick your finger through a skull's eye cavity, right up into the brain area. You cannot do that in the present state of affairs. Also. There now exists 4 or 6 small holes in the human skull that were never there before.

After I discovered large numbers of other physical changes to the human body, I knew what to think, friends: We're in new bodies.

What about the heart? Put your hand on your heart, like pledging allegiance to the flag. You will all place your right-hand way over to the left, because the heart WAS way over to the left. It now (records have always shown) is positioned near center and only slightly to the left. Amazing. Our muscle-memory isn't wrong. Everyone, in the history of the human race, has gotten it wrong? No. *It moved.* I watched an old film from 1939 recently and the guy pointed to the heart on an X-ray photo. Where the heart is and where the man pointed was almost dead center. If the heart was always/always near center, we'd be placing our hand near center. We don't.

The cerebellum has moved up more into the skull. There's been a change with the brain stem.

There's a different shoulder configuration we all share now. One section has three bones, where it was a single bone before. A report stated what was once a single part has been split in two. The clavicle bone is angled slightly differently.

The kidneys were low, but now they've moved up into the rib cage. Boxers' "kidney punches" were always low. Today, they'd punch in the wrong place.

The rib cage is larger. The liver is larger: *I suppose we can handle more alcohol in the dark world?* Also, the lungs are a bit smaller.

The diaphragm is larger and complex.

I don't know one Fallopian tube from another. But I believed the nurse when she declared: "The female reproductive organs are arranged a little differently now." *I don't want to know about the male organs.*

Look into this, do your own research. See for yourself what has changed. If you can?

70.   In Star Trek Next Generation, did Captain Jean Luc Picard have a handheld, polished crystal on his desk in the Ready Room, or not?

☯   Mandela people are confused by an advertisement where you can purchase the quartz piece, like Picard had in "78 episodes," for a few hundred dollars. A new marketing ploy or was it true? There are pics and quick clips of it on the show, online, that did not convince me. I thought they were computerized. I sure don't remember the Captain twiddling with a fidget item on his desk (78 episodes!) and I've seen every STNG show at least ten times each over decades. Many people have searched for the elusive crystal, only to report: "We haven't seen it."

Guess what, trekkers? I found the crystal in a few shows after Wesley got his Star Fleet uniform. It was in the climactic, 2-parter, end of 3rd Season, where Picard got assimilated by the Borg, called: 'Best of Both Worlds.' *Isn't that an interesting title, to maybe what's going on with the Mandela?* The crystal was also in the episode: 'Suddenly Human.' Here's what I think: There's been a crossover of mirror-worlds. Maybe Picard never had it in our universe, but did in the other, and you could buy it! It might be in the process of popping up in our STNG episodes? Who knows? I wouldn't be surprised that, presto, chango...*the "crystal was always there"* and might really make an appearance in 78 shows, eventually.

71.   Hey, you old guys and gals, remember the 1960s, the Beatles and the British bands that came to America in the first music invasion? Do any of you remember the first "answer" to the Beatles, long before 'Beatlemania,' called "The American Beetles"? I'm sure you recall them on Dick Clark's 'American Bandstand,' yes? Even Chuck Berry appeared on a 45 they recorded. Don't you recall one or two of their hits? Anyone?

☮   How can you seniors not remember the American Beetles' Argentina tour and their big hits? Hits like: 'Hey, Hey Girl,' 'Don't be Unkind' and the one Chuck Berry must have sold to them called, 'School Days.' It ripped off Chuck's 'No Particular Place to Go,' note for note. Seriously, you don't remember? *How could you?* The American Beetles (one more time for the Mandela) just popped into existence with a history that goes back to the early 1960s. They told Dick Clark they'd met the real Beatles and they were cool about the tribute band. *C'mon!* No lawsuits? In this reality: Did every country have their version, like the Jamaican Beetles? German Beetles? How about this? The Japanese Beetles! [I'm so funny]. This is in no one's memory, but we are faced with a long history of 'The American Beetles,' *like the bugs?* Did they have a beet on the record label, instead of an apple?

72.   In Mr. Rogers' opening song, does he sing: "It's a beautiful day in this neighborhood."? Are those the exact words he sings or not?

☮   Mr. Rogers never sang "THIS." It was 'the.' 'This' is not in the theme song. But now it is and I guess has *always been there?* It sounds wrong because it is different from what it was.

73.   In 'Under the Bridge,' maybe the best-known song by the Red Hot Chili Peppers, Anthony Kiedis sings about Los Angeles: Does he sing, "...The city she loves me, the City of Angel."? Or does he sing, "...The City of Angels."?

☮   Once again, the usual answer is wrong today. Been changed. LA is the "City of Angels," not the "City of Angel." He'd know better. It always was "Angels." LA people heard the song on KROQ a thousand times. We saw the music video of him singing it in the street. Play the original recording and the dude sings: "Angel." We've only found out about this now? Yes. All the real and stunning, mind-blowing, Mandela changes, *we've only found out about recently, in the last few years?* Not before? Isn't that peculiar?

74.   Speaking of KROQ, here is an absolute Mandela or real change from an obscure '80s band called the 'Violent Femmes' (prophetic title). Their big hit was called: "Blister in the Sun." Does singer Gordon Gano ever sing: "...A blister in the Sun."? Don't you recall that he did?

❧   The chorus of the song has been beat into any old KROQ listener and others who remember '80s Alternative Music. Today. You'd be wrong if you said the singer sang: "A blister..." Nope. Check it on YT. It's now transitioned into a *suntan commercial!* He sings: "I blister in the Sun." "I̲ blister in the Sun."? Microscopic changes, but real changes, in lyrics often have the same meaning. Not in this case. *Give him some lotion.* Strange that a YT video with written lyrics of the song was 'residue' and wrote out "A," while on the audio, simultaneously, was heard "I."

75.   What does Mick Jagger of the Rolling Stones sing in the song: 'Paint it, Black'? Is the correct lyric: "I see a red door and I want to paint it black..."? Or. "I see a red door and I want it painted black..."?

❧   Seems so small, doesn't it? The line really means the same and it's the same way with other tiny, subtle Mandela changes. Some are hardly noticeable and others are massive in scale and size. Stones have always been dark with 'Sympathy for the Devil.' Red doors are good and ward off negative spirits, legends tell. Painting a red one black cannot be good and might let in...demons? The first lyric was the old one that everyone remembers. Second lyric is new version on all recordings that no one remembers. (Yet, 'devils' may remember it's always been this way?). The point, again is, *nothing should have changed.* It is not our bad memories that are off and we've miss-remembered. Classic songs, movies, etc. have actually transformed, like magic. Was it at their 'Satanic Majesty's Request'? [I'm so good]. As I just checked, the magical/mystical album by the Rolling Stones *has changed titles,* in my opinion. Now it is called: "Satanic Majesties Request." Plural? And 'Paint It Black' suddenly has a comma.

76.   The pop band Aqua had one big hit and it was: 'Barbie Girl.' Does she sing, "I'm a Barbie Girl, in a Barbie world.''?

☯️   Yes. She does or did. Most all remember the line as in "a" Barbie world. Been changed. Play the video. She sings, "...In THE Barbie world." Small difference, but is it really so small? What is a Barbie World, the world of modeling, one that's fake, like acting and 'The Matrix'? Each M.E. confirms the other. We're only aware of these differences now or recently? How can that be? The uncomfortable truth is because the negative *"magic Reboot"* has only happened in the last few years.

77.   The old comedy team of Stan Laurel and Oliver Hardy had a catch phrase. What was it? It was in every movie and short film. Did the fat guy say to skinny guy: "That's another fine mess you've gotten me into."?

☯️   Simply take the opposite of what you'd normally think. *Of course Hardy didn't say what we all remember or it wouldn't be included as a Mandela!* See, if nothing's going on, then a minority of people would have remembered the classics wrong. That's not it. The great majority seems to remember wrong. Nope, *they remember right.* It's changed. Check YT. Not 'Mandela' YTs in this case. There are compilations of Laurel and Hardy's best scenes, from almost 90 years ago. See what the catch phrase is now. Should I tell you? A little advice: You should find out for yourself. Okay, I'll tell you. It's "NICE." The altered catch phrase on all movies and shorts of L&H is now, "That's another nice mess you've gotten me into." I watched their 1930 short film called: "ANOTHER FINE MESS." When the phrase was said, guess what was said? Not the title.

Now there's a new movie with Steve Coogan as Stan Laurel and John C. Reilly as Oliver Hardy (2018). It was all British. It completely jumped over their career and centered on a final tour in England. I only watched to hear the mutation of the classic line into the new line. Sure as shooting, the moment came and it was:

"Another nice mess you've gotten me into." Why do this movie? Because... Again, they are 'rubbing our face in the poopoo' mess they've created in the *real* world.

78. "A man's gotta do what a man's gotta do." Does that sound familiar, the phrase said by John Wayne in 'Hondo'?

❂ Wrong again, Pilgrim. Wouldn't you think that was Duke's famous line? Sure has been mimicked a million times. It was. Now look and it's (not) always been: "A man oughta do what he thinks is best." What? No lie. Let's study the difference closer. He *was* saying: A man knows what's right and you should do the right thing. *No longer,* not in the upside-down world. Now. You do WHATEVER, whatever you frikking think is best. Again, the trend is to denigrate the "man." Also to: "Do as thou wilt." (No matter who you hurt?).

79. Does the Cheshire Cat in the animated 'Alice in Wonderland' from 1951 say: "We're all mad here."? Or does he say: "Most everyone's mad here."?

❂ People remember the Disney classic and it was, "We're all mad here." There's residue on T-shirts, buttons and other products with the line: "We're all mad here." Is there meaning to the little change? Are they saying a few (darkly) illuminated people know there's a method to the madness? They believe they're not mad. (Crowded House: 'For the World and not the War': *"...And they believe their own dark medicine, believing it's good...").*

80. In 'Alice in Wonderland,' what was on top of the caps worn by Tweedle Dee and Tweedle Dum, flags or propellers?

❂ I remember propellers and so do the majority of people. Again, we're mostly all wrong. It's flags, today. Kids in the '50s wore beanie caps and some of them actually had propellers. None of them had flags. Was "play" exchanged for "patriotism"?

81. Can you believe that classic lines we are extremely familiar with (because we've heard them correctly a thousand times), such as: "Romeo, O Romeo, wherefore art thou?" "A day that will live

in infamy" and "I did! I did see a puddy tat!" no longer exist, said precisely that way?

☯ Would it really surprise you this far into a bogus M.E. Test? A test designed to present on a "tray," oddities or points in our grid matrix that just do not add up, anymore. If the Beatles and Mr. Rogers have been morphed, why not Shakespeare? We all remember the immortal lines uttered by Juliet on the balcony (window?). It was "Romeo, O Romeo"...now changed to: "O Romeo, Romeo." It was never that, but now it is on all versions of 'Romeo and Juliet.' I checked. The film with Laurence Harvey stated the new version. The movie with Leo DiCaprio and Claire Danes (Claire Danes?) said it. And the pretty Olivia Hussey now expresses the new line, which sounds odd to our ears. But *is* correct inside the different 'game' that's fallen upon us, like we're characters in 'Reboot.' It's how the Bard has always written the line. What? *Everyone was wrong for hundreds of years?* "All the world's a stage." Now, it is.

Franklin Delano Roosevelt's famous speech he gave the country after the bombing of Pearl Harbor, has changed. We would not forget well-known movie lines or big speeches in history. The great majority of people should remember the quote was: "A day that will live in infamy." December 7th. Any old veteran could tell you that. Now check the records, play FDR's speech on YouTube. The altered line or timeline is: "A date that will live in infamy." "Date," not "day."

Similarly, we're not going to forget the unforgettable line said by Tweedy Bird. Said over and over again by Tweedy. One more time, everyone is way off (no, they're not), because the changed quote is now: "I did! I did saw a puddy tat!"

82. If you're not a believer, a Mandela-person, you should be by now. Speaking of "What is truth?" Are you researchers aware of the change in the film: 'A Few Good Men'?

☯ Most of us remember: (Tom) "I want the truth." (Jack) "You want the truth? You can't handle the truth!" When you replay the film now, it is a little different from what we mainly remember: (Jack) "You want answers?" (Tom) "I want the truth." (Jack) "You can't handle the truth!" *I don't think we can~*

83.   In the film 'Back to the Future,' do you remember a small, gray figure of Doc (Christopher Lloyd) hanging from one of the many clocks in the opening sequence?

☯   Why would filmmakers be that stupid to foreshadow a big moment that will happen later in the film? People do not recall a tiny figure of Doc on a clock exactly like the real guy was positioned much later. There's one now. The clocks are very odd to my memory: One has "IIII" and not "IV." It's top number is "X" (10) and not 12. Numerals have shifted toward the right, like on a dial. A black clock has only 10 numbers with "10" at the top. The numbers went counterclockwise. Does '10 numbers instead of 12' refer to Time speeding up?

Later, we see a possibly changed VW van (some say). We view both versions of the Volkswagen logo?

[In the film, there's a photo that changed according to how events happened. In 'Dark City,' it was a book that changed. Also, a similar situation was in 'Frequency'].

84.   Do you have the feeling or sense that Time is speeding up? Do days and weeks fly by faster, or not?

☯   I sure get the sense that Time's moving faster. Is it accelerating? Daily routines that I logically know occur every 24 hours seem to happen in a much shorter span of time: *maybe 15 or 20 hours each cycle and not every 24 hours?* The good news is my Social Security checks come much sooner than monthly and TV commercials speed by in a minute! The bad news is life is racing by. It's how it seems to me.

Then to find a great many others also feel the same sensation or reality is comforting, I guess. All in the same boat, yes? Mandela Effect has been blamed as the agent that has sped up the clock. Try what they report:

Count the old way to ten seconds: "One Mississippi...two Mississippi...three..." If you time it, almost invariably, 12 seconds or more have passed by. Clocks could really be moving faster than our memory of how Time used to pass, a bit slower.

85.   Did Mickey Mouse have suspenders? Did Donald Duck have white spots on his shirt? Did Curious George have a tail? Did Pokémon's Pikachu have black on his tail? Did Mighty Mouse have an "M" on his chest?

☯   The correct answers yesterday were: yes, yes, yes, yes and yes. Correct answers today are: no, no, no, no and no.

86.   Have you noticed the odd position of jets on wings or do you believe there is nothing out-of-the-ordinary with the look of jet planes today?

☯   The conical, turbo things, under the wings of jet planes, were never in those positions before. Why would they be pushed so far out in front like headlights? Jet thrusters are no longer under the wings, *where they were.* Of course, the FAA would say: "They've always been there." I'm sure there is (now) a full history of them there, from early jets to modern planes. Yes, jets can fly with thusters way out in front, but why do that? It makes no sense since they would be more securely fastened right under the wing. *I think a child could design them better, with the jets pulled back.* They will, certainly, continue building jet planes somewhat differently from our memories.

87.   What do you remember was marked on car mirrors? Was it: "Objects in mirror are closer than they appear."? Or: "Objects in mirror may be closer than they appear."?

☯   I'd say "may be closer than they appear." That rings a bell for me. Again, the true answer now is: "Objects in mirror are closer than they appear." No "maybes" about it in the new version. They are definitely closer. And, possibly, so is the whole universe? (The Sun is white? Thought it was yellow?).

88.   The color chartreuse, is it rose-colored or green in color? What would you say?

☯   Many people distinctly remember the color chartreuse being rose-colored. I think I do as well. But now it's green-colored. Even a French liqueur of same name, made by Carthusian monks, apparently, has turned green and has always been green in color. I'd imagine the rose color would've been better-looking for the wine.

89.   How many people were in JFK's motorcade when he was shot, 4 or 6?

☯   When this was questioned, in the beginning of studying the M.E., I was amazed and thought: *How could anyone ever get this wrong?* Or 'The Thinker' statue? Or the Lindbergh baby and even the original Mandela Effect: Nelson did not die in prison! *Or did he?* But after viewing more and more, an endless stream of weeding out nonsense from real Mandelas, I've concluded...

Most all of us in our collective memory might have every record book in our favor, every stat, fact and figure, photograph and film documentary could support our view. That doesn't mean a freaking thing, anymore, apparently. Because there's someone over there or a minority group of people or a majority group of people who distinctly remember differently. Maybe they're not wrong, crazy, ignorant or delusional? Maybe they come from another experience, another history and worlds are truly intersecting? Do we switch from one polarity to another? One ancient or recent history to another?

People remember six: the Kennedys in back, the two feds in front and Governor Connally and his wife in the middle. The "magic bullet" struck the governor in the wrist, remember? Yet, oddly enough: There is evidence, photos, documents, etc. that show only four! Four? If so, this could be a crossover. In the parallel world, there must only have been four. In another universe that I remember, there were 6 in the motorcade.

I've learned to not be so hasty to demand *this is right and this is wrong,* these days.

90.   Do you agree with the official record that the Challenger Shuttle disaster happened in January of 1986? Or do you remember that it occurred at an earlier date?

☯   With this one I feel in the big minority here, yet certain of my facts. Probably, most people would not contest the historical record of 1/1986. Like my Moon-marker, I have a memory-marker with the Shuttle disaster. If you have a strong memory (such as with Jiffy or C3PO) no one is ever going to take that away. I heard about this from a researcher who was in HS at the time. Most teachers were instructed to have their classes watch. This was because the first private citizen, a teacher, was onboard. [Was it not an accident? Instructing teachers to show children what was going to happen?]. It was a powerfully traumatic experience for the kid at the time. He remembered the class and exactly where he was when the disaster happened. It was his '84 to '85 year class.

This perfectly jives with my memory. I discussed the disaster with a friend at the time. He moved away late 1984, definitely. From my recollection, the explosion couldn't have happened in 1986 or even 1985. Who knows? It could be one way in one world and a distorted reflection in the other world?

This book does not examine the idea that people we thought had died, apparently, did not. Sure, mistaken memories. Someone is out of the spotlight or very old and we think they're deceased. Billy Graham and a long list of others, I guess, weren't dead after all. But. Maybe they were...in one world? And lived to a different age in another?

91.   The curious case of Ed McMahon and Publisher's Clearing House Sweepstakes. What's the vote? Did Ed work for PCH or not?

❧   Maybe it exists one way in one world and another way in the alternative world? There is so much residue evidence that Ed McMahon once was the voice of PCH, did ads for them and even was there at the door with balloons, champagne and a big check. He was known for that to many people, as well as Dick Clark. Both did ads together, vividly etched into the public's memory. They remember, "Ed said, you may already be a winner." Johnny Carson appeared on the Letterman Show in '91, gave Dave a large Publisher's Clearing House check for a million dollars and apologized that Ed couldn't be here. The references of people hoping to win the million bucks from Ed are endless. There's only one conclusion, ladies and gentleman: In one world, he did.

In the Dark Side, meta-morphed world of today, things have

changed. Records have changed. *Presto, chango*...everyone's wrong because Ed and Dick Clark never, never worked for PCH. They want us to believe people are simply confused and have mistaken PCH with the American Family Publisher's sweepstakes that began in 1977. Ed and Dick did work for AFP, *but never PCH?* Ah, that was only in one universe. Now, considering the Mandela, our world's been altered to one where Ed only worked for little-known AFP and never for famous Publisher's Clearing House. It seems the world where he was employed by PCH is now gone. In one world, he did. In another, he did not.

92.   Are you aware of a connection between the film 'The Matrix Reloaded' and the Bible passage: Isaiah 54/16?

☯   As one researcher discovered: "The Matrix is in the Bible and the Bible is in the Matrix." Isaiah 54/16 now states:
     "Behold, I have created **smith** that bloweth the coals in the fire, and that bringeth forth an instrument for his work; and I have created the waster to destroy."
     That is one of countless strange Bible verses that have suddenly appeared, along with a lot of satanic things. Now view 'The Matrix Reloaded.' One particular shot has a license plate that reads: "IS 5416," the precise verse that calls "smith" a "waster," a destroyer...like he was in the film. Why couldn't biblical 'smith' be good? No, he's bad guy. Coincidence?

93.   In the Bible, Isaiah 11:6, what sleeps or lays with the Lamb, the Lion or the Wolf?

☯   Yes, even the King James Bible has altered. No surprise, but a shock once you read the new version. It used to be the Lion who laid with the Lamb, now it's the Wolf. It's an expression and also has been the subject of numerous paintings that represented peace. The lion doesn't eat the lamb. *I'll bet the wolf does.* Exact new quote is: "The wolf also shall dwell with the lamb..." What does it mean? Why the change? Wolf is a royal symbol and one of fascism. Anti-Christ? Unfortunately, good people, the KJV has been corrupted and has turned into the **Dark Bible**, its evil twin.

94.   In the Lord's Prayer, Matthew 6:10, is it "on earth as it is in

heaven"? Or is it "in earth as it is in heaven"?

❧   The "correct" reference in the Lord's Prayer, or the way it was, was: "...On earth as it is in heaven." Something's obviously changed the Bible and the physical world because the well-known phrase now reads: "...In earth as it is in heaven." Two 'in's. What does 'in earth' mean? We live *on Earth.* Does it mean a shift to where those in future must live underground? Are they making bunkers like heaven?

Mandela people are fascinated with "residue," bits of evidence that prove the way it was, such as an old coupon for "JIFFY" peanut butter. Truth is we know how it was, we remember. Fascinating, are the *changes* (to me). I started to watch an old movie ('Black Friday') just to get away from the Mandela research, and *I couldn't.* It's everywhere! A priest led Boris Karloff out of jail to be executed. He spoke the 'Lord's Prayer.' I jumped to attention and carefully listened. The priest miss-quoted the line: He said "IN," twice. "...In Earth as it is in heaven." The priest character, from 1940, didn't get the verse wrong. That's what the line is now in the Dark Bible, in the changed world and its changed history. If a letter in the Bible has unnaturally changed, so can continents. And they have.

Also in the Lord's Prayer, it was: "And forgive us our trespasses, as we forgive those who trespass against us." The classic line has been changed to: "Forgive us our debts, as we also have forgiven our debtors."

95.   One of the Ten Commandments is: "Honour thy mother and thy father." Was it the Fourth Commandment, or was it the Fifth?

❧   We will dig deeply into this important question: **Have the Commandments changed in the King James Bible?** Here is another I found all on my own and not from any Mandela researcher. I wondered, "These first Laws of Moses that we all should know well, had they altered like other verses in the Bible and things everywhere?" I looked for a small word-change. I went online, Google, and kept scanning every reference out there of the Ten Commandments. Such as:

1. Thou shalt have no other gods before me.

2. Thou shalt not make unto thee any graven image.
3. Thou shalt not take the name of the Lord thy God in vain.
4. Remember the sabbath day, to keep it holy.
5. Honour thy father and thy mother.
6. Thou shalt not kill.
7. Thou shalt not commit adultery.
8. Thou shalt not steal.
9. Thou shalt not bare false witness against thy neighbor.
10. Thou shalt not covet thy neighbor's house, wife, etc.

Another listing was more modern, called: 'Short Summary of the 10 Commandments':
1. Do not have any other God before God.
2. Do not make yourself an idol.
3. Do not take the Lord's name in vain.
4. Remember the sabbath day and keep it holy.
5. Honor your mother and father.
6. Do not murder.
7. Do not commit adultery.
8. Do not steal.
9. Do not bare false witness against your neighbor.
10. Do not covet.

On 'The Ten Commandments' monument in Goshon, Ohio, carved into stone are almost the same words written on the 'Summary.' Small differences are: "...no other gods before me" and "...not worship any graven image."

Notice that in these online examples and (apparently) every example or reference to them these days, THE ORDER IS DIFFERENT than what they used to be. I was curious if a *word* was different; I didn't expect an *alteration in the Commandments chronological order!* You don't remember? Maybe you haven't spotted the change? Certainly, older, Bible scholars would have seen it in two seconds. Hang on.

Now, there is all the reason in the world to believe the many references today have it precisely right, because the Bible backs up this (new) order. The following are exact quotes from the King James:

Exodus 20/1: And God spoke all these words, saying,

2: I am the LORD thy God, which have brought thee out of bondage.

3: Thou shalt have no other gods before me.

4: Thou shalt not make unto thee any graven image, or any likeness of anything that *is* in heaven above, or that *is* in the earth beneath, or that *is* in the water under the earth:

5: Thou shalt not bow down thyself to them, nor serve them: for I the LORD thy God, visiting the iniquity of the fathers upon the children unto the third and fourth generation of them that hate me;

6: And **shewing** mercy unto thousands of them that love me, and keep my commandments.

7: Thou shalt not take the name of the LORD thy God in vain; for the LORD will not hold him guiltless that taketh his name in vain.

8: Remember the Sabbath, to keep it holy.

Another reference to: "...in the earth."?

The next three verses make little sense and seem like a recent alteration. In fact, all of the Commandments listed here, and in Deuteronomy, appear (to me) completely different. I remember a listing or listings, clearly written out in numerical order. But in Exodus and in Deuteronomy, where the Commandments are known to be printed, we have to pick the 10 out from verses. Verse numbers are not the Commandment numbers. The three verses repeat Genesis, of a cruel/ruthless "jealous" God, demanding obedience and servitude [to me, shows a tyrannical, megalomaniac God and therefore not the Supreme Being of goodness, love and mercy]. Sins of the father should never be visited upon the children, but this (Old World) "God" thinks descendants should be punished for 3 or 4 generations. In these strange verses, people are reminded what the sabbath is, to not work on that day; that God created the world in 6 days and rested on the seventh. I have no recollection of these repetitive 'speeches' by God within the list of Commandments, twice.

But consider the new order of Commandments that can be ascertained in the verses. Basically, 1: no other gods. 2: no idols. 3: don't cuss. And #4 is now: Remember Sunday, keep it holy. THAT'S NOT THE 4TH COMMANDMENT! Today, (about) all the references say it is and the Bible also says it is.

No it's not, folks.

If you were a Baby-Boomer, came from a family that took you to Church as a kid and you misbehaved, parents might throw in your face: "What's the fourth Commandment say? Honor your mother and father!" This scolding is clearly etched in my mind because of how often it was repeated and I'm sure in the minds of plenty of others who remember the old days. I am 100% sure it was always, always the 4th…but now, *black magically,* everyone in the world and the Bible itself will tell you…it's the fifth. I also think it was "mother and father," but now changed to "father and mother."

Verse 12: Honour thy father and thy mother: that thy days may be long upon the land, which the LORD thy God giveth thee.

13: Thou shalt not kill…

The rest of them are much as I remember. From my POV, it is like the fourth and fifth Commandments have switched places. Could there be a dark or demonic meaning in this Mandela Effect as well? The destruction or dissolution of the family, reinforced by almost every TV show, commercial and movie: bad parents, bad role models, bad children. Possibly the Dark Universe that appears to be physically changing things, has demoted the Parent-Commandment from 4 to 5 because it wants to end good families? It's just not important anymore to obey parents in a crazy, chaotic, 'do-as-thou-wilt' society. Is that the reason for the change?

Examine Exodus 20, verse 6, above. SHEWING? The word "showing" is misspelled; look at the context of the phrase. Other verses have "shew" or "shewn" when the words are clearly "show" and "shown." Many other words are misspelled as well as there now exists terrible grammatical errors that were never in the Bible previously. What is going on? This is 'Bad Bible' and not close to the one I remember. "Shalt" in the Commandments"? I thought it was: "Thou shall not...""?

96. What did baby Moses float down the Nile river in, a papyrus basket or an ark of bulrushes? Which one do you remember is more accurate?

☯ Let's take the answer directly from my mother's 90 year-old Bible, the one that's *now been changed (like all others)*. Let's follow Moses' birth and the events right after his birth:

Exodus 2/1: And there went a man of the house of Levi, and took *to wife* a daughter of Levi.

2: And the woman conceived, and bare a son: and when she saw him that he *was a goodly child,* she hid him three months.

3: When she could not longer hide him, she took for him an ark of bulrushes, and daubed it with slime and with pitch, and put the child therein; and she laid it in the flags by the river's brink.

The above verses in Exodus are very different and distorted than most everyone's recollection. The answer today is: Moses floated down the Nile in an "ark of bulrushes," but that surely is in no one's memory. We know of Moses' later association with the Ark of the Covenant. Another "ark" attached to him besides the Covenant? The Covenant, Noah's Ark and now a third "ark" in Bible? No way. We remember a "basket" of "papyrus" that was water-sealed with tar and pitch, not slime and pitch. *Slime?* There is a lot of residual evidence for "basket." "Bulrushes" "is a biblical term" that means *papyrus,* but that is not what we remember. "Papyrus" was in many places in the King James. But in the Bible of this new universe, *it is nowhere to be found.*

"Took to wife" is a new reference in Moses' birth. "Bore" a son, but it is now "bare"? "Goodly child"? I thought it was "beautiful child"? "Flags" seem to represent "reeds" along the Nile shore. "River's brink" sounds wrong and probably was originally: "along the bank of the Nile river." "When she could not longer hide him." What incorrect English! Who was the idiot that translated this bizarre Bible? Some of the changed words are similar (brink/bank, flags/reeds). Is it merely a matter of different translations from the Mirror Universe? *Maybe we're now that other world,* where the transcribers didn't really care that much about what they were doing? In 'The Ten Commandments' (1956), Moses' journey down the Nile is portrayed in Technicolor...the word "ark" is used once, instead of "basket."

97.   Were Adam and Eve married?

❧   Here is the new line in Genesis 2/25: And they were both naked, the man and his **wife**, and were not ashamed.

There wouldn't have been one Bible scholar that could point to proof of the marriage between Adam and Eve, previously. Now,

Bible scholars must because: *there it is in Genesis.* Who performed the ceremony?

98. Was Jesus born outside, in a manger? Or, was he born in a house?

❧   I thought there was no room at the inn? You mean the art, imagery, plays, films and large number of portrayals of Christ's birth were in holy error? Yes, for centuries. Apparently that's the case, today. No one "on Earth" would ever have thought that before the Mandela Effect. Read the verses in the KJV...

Matthew 2/9: When they had heard the king, they departed; and, lo, the star, which they saw in the east, went before them, till it came and stood over where the young child was.

2/10: When they saw the star, they rejoiced with exceeding great joy.

2/11: And when they were come into the **house**, they saw the young child with Mary his mother, and fell down, and worshipped him: and when they had opened their treasures, they presented unto him gifts, gold and frankincense, and myrrh.

So much has been changed of the KJV that it is no longer the "King James," as you will read. The Good Book has turning into the Bad Book, changed into the Dark Bible, right on our shelves, with a wave of a magic 'wand.'

99.   The following words were either *always* in the Bible or *never* in the Bible? Which is the answer? Addicted, advertise, ambassage, aliens, artillery, bestead, bethink, betimes, bullrushes, butler, carriage, castle, chapiter, charger, closet, cockatrice, collops, communication, commune, compass, couch, countervail, damsel, darling, Dodo, dragons, drams, duke, Easter, emerods, environ, estate, fan, fanners, feller, ferry boat, froward, frowardness, furniture, glittering spear, goodlier, goodliest, gutter, habergeon, helve, horseleech, hough, inventions, intermeddleth, Jupiter, killedst, kine, king's court, lade, leasing, liquor, lionlike men, listeth, Lucifer, magnifical, mansions, Mars, menservant, merchantman, mete, meteyard, minished, minister, munition, necromancer, noisome, ouches, overcharged, palace, pastor, plat, platted, pilled, pommels, princess, princesses, printed, privily,

purtenance, residue, rentest, reprobate, roebuck, royal, satyr, Seed of David, senators, shamefacedness, shittah, shittim, snuffed, soldier, space, station, stonesquarers, straiten, stuff, suburbs, suits, tabret, taches, target, teil tree, traffick, unicorn, usury, vagabond, void, waster, wench, wine bottles, wist, witch, wizard, worthies, wot...

☙   Just look at the above words; *look again!* Are these biblical words or are these words out of 'Game of Thrones'? Do these words describe things thousands of years ago or do they describe a world of 500 years ago? How many are totally unfamiliar to you and make little sense? This is the English language and the words are butchered. A good portion of these words have never been seen before. Wouldn't we know them if they were found in the Bible?

They were never in the pages of "Holy Scripture." Never. Take the word of Bible scholars who are outraged ever since the Mandela Wave struck and the KJV morphed. Every word on the list are now in the Bible and they never were before.

100.   In the introduction to the KJV of the Bible, there are two pages under the large-lettered heading of "**JAMES**." In the preface, which consists of 6 paragraphs, do you remember the name of Her Highness, **Queen Elizabeth** [standing Queen of England] being mentioned in very old Bibles? Could it be possible that even a hundred year-old copy of the King James specifically states Elizabeth's name as Sovereign of Britain and future Queen though she is in her nineties, today?

☙   NO! Impossible! Closely examine the first 2 pages of intro, 6 paragraphs, that precede Genesis under heading of 'JAMES.' The following are the exact titles, first paragraph and parts of other paragraphs in what is an absolutely new preface! These words were never there before, now they begin every King James Bible (everywhere):

TO THE MOST HIGH AND MIGHTY PRINCE
JAMES
BY THE GRACE OF GOD.
KING OF GREAT BRITAIN, FRANCE
AND IRELAND.

DEFENDER OF THE FAITH, ETC.

The translators of the Bible wish Grace, Mercy and Peace,
through JESUS CHRIST our Lord.

GREAT and manifold were the blessings, **most dread Sovereign**, which Almighty God, the Father of all mercies, bestowed upon us the people of *England,* when first he sent Your Majesty's Royal Person to rule and reign over us. For whereas it was the expectation of many who wished not well unto our *Sion,* that upon the setting of that bright *Occidental Star,* **Queen Elizabeth** of most happy memory, some thick and palpable clouds of darkness would so have overshadowed this Land, that men should have been in doubt which way they were to walk; and that it should hardly be known, who was to direct the unsettled State; the appearance of **Your Majesty, as of the *Sun* in his strength**, instantly dispelled those supposed and surmised mists, and gave unto all that were well affected exceeding cause of comfort; especially when we beheld the Government established in Your Highness, and Your hopeful Seed, by an undoubted title, and this also accompanied with peace and tranquility at home and abroad.

Let's analyze the first paragraph, which certainly mentions current Queen of England. ***This is impossible!*** Very old Bibles predate the very existence of Elizabeth. She had nothing to do with the Bible. Queen Victoria had nothing to do with the Bible. LIZ CAN'T FUCKING BE WRITTEN IN THE BIBLE AND SHE DAMN WELL IS! How could very old Bibles have a different KJ preface? They couldn't; they don't. They all have these *different, warped* words now. This is a 100% total contradiction, a living unicorn staring you in the face! What're you going to do about it? Show others the impossibility in your hand or bury it and do nothing? Just pretend it's not there? Or say: *"It's always been there."*?

The first sentence informs us that a merciful God has given us a **"most dread Sovereign,"** which is Queen Liz. 'Most dread' is not good. They are telling you, in plain sight, she's a beast, a monster (like many have revealed about the Monarchy in recent years). Sion is Zion, Zionism: not good. 'Occidental Star' means of European ancestry. 'State' and 'Government' couldn't have been in the original preface, but the modern words are there now. 'Your Majesty, as of the *Sun* in his strength.' Every time earth, moon and sun are written in the Bible, they are not capitalized. 'Sun' is here; does it mean pagan Sun-worship? 'His strength'? The Sun or the (male) Queen? 'Seed' is royal bloodlines. *Queen Elizabeth is honored more than Jesus or God!* I thought God ('He') was capitalized in the Bible? Not in the intro. Also strange that 'holy' Truth, 'holy' Scriptures are not capitalized, and yet, *everything* is capitalized and overstated when it comes to the Queen.

The second paragraph of the intro ends: "...to the time spent in this **transitory world**, but directeth and desposeth men unto that eternal happiness which is above in heaven." *A world in transition or is it a world of trannies?*

The third paragraph in the intro ends: "...by hearing the Word preached, by cherishing the Teachers thereof by caring for the Church, as a most tender and loving **nursing father**." Speaking of trannies, you'll find that the royalty are and have been trans-gendered. Now we have a royal abomination right at the very beginning. Fathers do not nurse. But they do in the trans-gendered world of elites who are apparently rewriting the Bible in their own dark image.

The fourth paragraph of the Bible's new preface or foreword ends with: "...there should be one more exact Translation of the holy Scriptures into the *English Tongue;* Your Majesty did never desist to urge to excite those to whom it was commended, that the work might be hastened, and that the business might be expedited in so decent a manner, as a matter of such importance might justly require." We need one more 'exact Translation'? The KJ was the first! This is the first in English, not another one. 'Business'? They're telling you the truth. The Church of England, like the Vatican, is money, a global business.

The fifth paragraph ends: "...and sustained without by the powerful protection of Your Majesty's grace and favour, which, will ever give countenance to honest and christian endeavours against bitter censures and uncharitable imputations."

The start of the sixth and last paragraph in the Bible's introduction: "The Lord of heaven and earth bless Your Majesty with many and happy days, that, as his heavenly hand hath enriched Your Highness with many singular and extraordinary graces, so You may be the wonder of the world in this latter age..."

Wow. What a fucking crock of shit! *God has blessed Queen Elizabeth with "extraordinary" superpowers?* And we all may be 'the wonder of the world'? It's beyond extraordinary. These are extraordinary lies. It's "sick," which is not a compliment.

Wouldn't you think if the Illuminati wanted to push a new, perverse Bible of Satan...it would've hired a staff of writers, controlled a Media firestorm and the Devil's Bible would be *flying off the shelves* in all major bookstores? No, that's not what happened. Scientific Black Magic happened. Someone opened a portal to a world of evil or *something* because everything has negatively changed. A 'magical wand' was waved ("Order 66") and abracadabra...all the King James versions as well as some other modern Bibles have "supernaturally" changed, been rewritten and pushed to the Dark Side. Like almost everything else. Who'd believe it?

One more change is this is *not the King James' Bible anymore.* It's the translation of **"PRINCE James."** Look at the intro's title page again. Since when was he only a PRINCE when the Bible was translated into English? Only a king could order the translation. Prince James is referred to as "The Most High and Mighty." Are you sure this is the same King James Bible that your parents and grandparents had? *It's not.*

Critics of this view say it is not Elizabeth II mentioned, it was Elizabeth I. She was the queen who died and made James of Scotland king of Britain. Problem is she had nothing to do with the English Bible. It was under the authority of King James, much later. "Elizabeth I" is not there in print, only "Queen Elizabeth." It would be "JAMES" praised over and over in the intro of his name, not any Elizabeth. King James was never Prince James.

Don't you see what dark wizards have done to the world? Proof is right in front of you and all around you. You only have to open your eyes, your reluctant eyes.

Who wants to believe any of this?

One more change to consider is what has occurred to the Shroud of Turin...

Jesus Christ's burial cloth is absolutely real, always been real. Carbon 14 has always been an inaccurate measuring stick for dating anything. It is perfect for educational systems that don't want you educated (like Darwin Evolution). They want you to believe items that are extremely old, that don't fit the historical picture they've laid out, *are not that old at all.* "Take the date Carbon 14 gives you and multiply it by 3 or more, then you'll get an accurate date." I've said this long before the Shroud was "dated" decades ago, and knew the figure would be a great underestimate. There is all the reason in the world for "scientists" to *not want* the cloth to be 2000 years old. If they used reliable dating methods, the Turin Shroud would be 2000 years old.

The linen is the exact material for burial shrouds in that area and at that time. The exact number of lashes on the back of the man on the Shroud is stated in the Bible and in movies (39). The spear wound in the side is accurately displayed on the cloth. The man wore a cap of thorns and not a crown of thorns. Blood flows on the material show real patterns due to gravity. Man on the Shroud (I believe) is Jesus. The best proof of the cloth's credibility are the wrist wounds. We believe, because of stigmata imagery and paintings down through the ages, that the wounds were in the palms of the hands. Not true. Tests on cadavers demonstrated bodies cannot be nailed up this way: the body's weight is too much and falls because hand bones are too small and fragile. But if nailed just below the wrists, a body can hang. It was where all people were nailed, crucified in this manner, through the wrists.

Visitors who have seen the Shroud view only a faint image on a white cloth. The 'miracle' occurs when we see the dark negative, *sharp details come alive!* The Shroud was damaged in 1532 by "a drop of molten silver," which burned through it while folded. In 1902, Secondo Pia was commissioned by the Pope to photograph the Shroud for the first time, as to preserve the image forever. When the photographer examined his negatives...that was the amazing part, the world first discovered such phenomenal pictures! I can't imagine what it would have been like for those who cared for the Shroud, to suddenly see it in the negative~

Was the mysterious Shroud image (not paint) caused by radiation? Something "scorched" or radiated through the linen? **How did a 2000-year old, photographic negative-image happen?** That's an old question. But now...

Mandela has changed everything into a doppelganger of

itself. In some cases, the changes have been horrific, a twisted version, a Hyde to a Dr. Jekyll. How could Michelangelo have done what he done to the (new, added) Sistine Chapel and also put *horns on Moses?* Well, people, all this lead-in was to inform you that now...there seems to be an addition to Jesus' burial cloth. Possibly "horns." Horns, again? An odd thingee has appeared right above the man's head that people don't remember and has been described as "horns." Spooky. When I examined photos of the Turin Shroud negative today, the man looks a bit like an *insect.* I never noticed that previously.

One more Mandela change I've noticed ONLY NOW! It occurred when I looked up Secondo Pia! See above. I wrote the famous photos were taken in 1902. [I'm leaving that there because it WAS true]. **It *was* in my reality, but not in today's version. "1902" came from a vivid memory as well as the details on the Shroud I knew. Nothing had to be looked up. I've talked about the Shroud decades ago and in the last 15 years on at least one radio show. That is no longer the date that Secondo Pia photographed the cloth and noticed his negative. Wow, *who knew that's been changed?* I only found out at this moment. I expected the record to report it was 1902. I am not wrong. The world is now. 1898? Four years earlier is when it was taken, in this universe. Unexpected. This is very similar to many other things and the Bible: The KJV was always published in 1612. Now the date of publication is 1611?**

Everything is just a little different...

Why not one more for good measure?

101. In the movie 'And Justice for All,' Al Pacino gave a strong performance and said very famous lines that we all remember. Or do we? When the judge yelled at him that he was *"Out of order,"* didn't he say: "I'm out of order? You're out of order! This whole courtroom is out of order!"?

☻ If you are up on your Mandelas, then you are aware those are no longer the words he screams in court. The new lines are: "You're out of order! You're out of order! The whole trial is out of order! They're out of..."

This could be of extreme importance in its meaning that the Mandela community has overlooked. Possibly. There is no Justice for all. Also. Look what's out of order these days? *EVERYTHING!*

Before I found the Mandela Effect and became obsessed by the oddities where 2 + 2 no longer added up to 4, I looked into what's only recently appeared in the last few years: Mud Floods, "re-sets" and the Tartarian or Tartary Empire. I was overwhelmed, the more I studied...

Incredible buildings, architecture, super city foundations and statues a few hundred years old? What? During Civil War times, people all over the planet constructed far superior structures than in the 20th Century? Buildings built better than today two centuries ago? Really? Architecture with spheres on top of towers where people have suggested the structures produced Tesla-like energies? Old fireplaces that weren't fireplaces, but conduits that generated wireless energy? Tesla-principles long before Tesla? No, no, no! *This never happened!* The man was 200 years ahead of his time. There was NOTHING like Tesla, before Tesla. I guess that's all wrong, today. Because you cannot deny endless black and white photos and films. These pictures of a so-called "Tartary" or "Tartarian Empire" never existed previously (before Mandela). What you'll see is technology that we never had until much later. I am of the mind now that this Tartaric New Age, no researcher has known until recently, is part of the Mandela. Like many other things, *it just appeared.*

You can view old photos of unbelievable statues, towers and buildings that will boggle the mind. Grand Romanesque figures, gargoyles and repeated patterns in tremendous detail all over the planet! We had previously believed everything that adorned great buildings was carved. But this "new" Tartarian architecture suggests pieces were cast because of the sheer repetition over such large areas. No one could have hand-carved the designs; they had to have been made from molds and pieced together. Towers reached to the sky. It's been suggested that these super buildings were destroyed on purpose so later generations would not discover that a *secret technology* had existed a few hundred years ago.

In the world I knew, there was one Great Flood that even covered Mt. Everest, 5000 years ago. But this new-history timeline now shows us that many "Mud Floods" have occurred that re-set humanity and tossed it back to a more primitive state. Photos show mud and lower sections of buildings and whole cities. The constructions on top, that came later, were not as advanced as the foundations from a much earlier age.

Where did this come from and why are we just hearing of it now? Could this be connected to Mandela in the same way the giant statues, "flying saucer" temple, islands and other changes seemed to have appeared out of nowhere?

I remembered a big error on the part of researchers that believed Tartary was always a part of our history and accounted for the amazing, monolithic constructions of the Egyptians, Incas and on and on and *every ancient civilization.* Bull. In my world, there were Lemurians, Atlanteans, Egyptians, Incas, Toltecs, Olmecs, Mayas, Aztecs, east Indian societies that flew and built utopias (until they fell and recycled) and great mound-builders. That full-spectrum of advanced human history cannot be eliminated by "Tartary" or Mandela. Or can it?

If we are within a New World, with a different (more advanced) history than the Old World, just a thought...

The Shroud being captured in photographs in 1898 rather than my recollection of 1902, almost makes a little sense. Technology was slightly more advanced in the Dark World, apparently, and made it possible for the historic Shroud photographs to happen earlier?

The sudden Tartaric Empire, amazing structures that were built hundreds of years ago, plus other oddities recently discovered, beyond what we normally thought were possible for the times, support the idea that...

In the new reality, we were slightly more advanced than in the Old World. The following are official years for the first photography of its kind:

1825 - First "heliographic" engraving (sun-camera).
1835 - Oldest existing camera negative.
1838 - Earliest known shot of people.
1839 - First self-portrait.
1840 - Earliest photo of a woman (very clear).

1840 - First detailed photograph of the Moon.

1845 - First photo of Sun, with sunspots.

1856 - First underwater photo.

1860 - First aerial photo, buildings of a city.

1861 - Earliest color photo.

1946 - First photo from space.

Doesn't it seem more advanced than it should be? Shouldn't the years be later for each development? It is possible that the dates have changed. These might not be the correct dates in the Lost World we used to live in? But they are the official records now.

Every field, every department, every stat has to be evaluated and questioned. Has there been a change or not?

*** Analysis of the Alternate Reality or New Timeline we are Within ~

☯ The following are mostly product name changes, incredible name changes! Design changes. *Companies wouldn't do that.* As stated earlier, companies have built brands over the course of decades. There would be no sane reason to, suddenly, change the brand name, misspell their own products? Rearrange a well-known logo? Why? So the vast market of people they've serviced or have used/consumed their products can scratch their heads and wonder: "What the heck? Do they not know the name of their product?"

EVERY item on the list is not an example of the Mandela Effect. I think a very large majority of them *are* real and true. They are surprising alterations in product names, designs, famous quotes, lines, lyrics, etc. that would not have happened if the Effect had not happened. Why do we say a product's name one way, when it's another way? Maybe we remember the old designs, titles, quotes and names, before they were transformed?

Products, companies, corporations, etc. have been researched; people have been contacted. Ninety-nine times out of a hundred, the official [truth in this reality] response is: "That's the way it's always been." But Old Worlders remember differently.

To repeat, these are not the usual upgrades and normal changes companies make to keep-up-with-the-times. Those are announced. These are inexplicable. We can research early images of a certain product we suspect has been altered and find it was *always the new way,* which is misspelled from the way we remember.

It's not necessarily an "evil plot" in each case of M.E. changes in the last few years. Theory is: "A dark, deadly, twin universe is descending upon us and changing things. It's now different here, here and over there." Changes in product names and logos, movie and music quotes, might simply be HOW IT IS in the negative universe that seems to be consuming/morphing everything that once was and also us who remember the Old World...

Fruit of the Loom underwear logo with fruit & cornucopia ==> Only fruit and no cornucopia.

Starbucks coffee cups, green and black logo on white cups with: 'STARBUCKS COFFEE' printed around image of the woman ==> only picture of the woman on cups without "Starbucks Coffee" on them.

Volvo logo that's only a circle ==> A male symbol, circle and arrow.

Volkswagen logo, no v/w separation ==> A line separates v/w.

Volkswagon ==> Volkswagen.

Ford logo without curly-Q on "F" ==> With curly-Q on "F."

Alpha Romero ==> Alpha Romeo.

Camero ==> Camaro.

Toyota Solaris ==> Toyota Solara.

Suburu ==> Subaru.

Mitzubishi ==> Mitsubishi.

Rolls Royce ==> Rolls-Royce.

No Corvette station wagons ==> A history of Corvette station wagons.

No 4-door Mustangs ==> A history of 4-door Mustangs.

Alaskan Airlines ==> Alaska Airlines.

Peterbuilt ==> Peterbilt.

Snap-on tools, no wrench in logo ==> Wrench in logo.

Louie Vuitton ==> Louis Vuitton.

Abercrombie and Finch ==> Abercrombie and Fitch.

Victoria Secret ==> Victoria's Secret.

Johnny Walker ==> Johnnie Walker.

Absolute ==> Absolut.

Bud Lite ==> Bud Light.

Coors Lite ==> Coors Light.

Michelobe ==> Michelob.

Anheiser Busch ==> Anheuser Busch.

Schwepps ==> Schweppes.

Nordstrom's ==> Nordstrom.

Siemen ==> Siemens.

Dupont ==> DuPont.

google ==> Google.
Twitter, normal small "t"s ==> Twitter, broken small "t"s.
20th Century Fox, normal small "t" in logo ==> Broken small "t" in logo.
ABC Entertainment, normal "b" ==> "b" is a circle on bottom.
GE ==> gE.
eBay ==> ebay.
IHops ==> Ihop.
Frigidaire, normal "a" ==> Red pyramid for an "a."
Legos ==> Lego.
Chuck E. Cheese ==> Chuck E. Cheese's.
Velveta ==> Velveeta.
Toast Cheese ==> Toast Chee.
Proctor and Gamble ==> Procter and Gamble.
MacDonalds ==> McDonalds ==> McDonald's.
Pollo Loco ==> El Pollo Loco.
Home Depot ==> The Home Depot.
The Olive Garden ==> Olive Garden.
The History Channel ==> History.
The Waffle House ==> Waffle House.
White Out ==> Wite Out.
Morton Salt ==> Morton's Salt.
Chic-fil-a ==> Chick-fil-a.
Tidy Bowl ==> Ty-D-Bol.
Tidy Cat ==> Tidy Cats.
Fabreeze, Fabreze, Febreeze ==> Febreze.
Rubix's Cube ==> Rubik's Cube.
Cliff's Notes, Cliff Notes ==> CliffNotes.
Oxy Clean ==> Oxi Clean.
Cup 'O' Noodles ==> Cup Noodles.
Depends ==> Depend.
Cosco ==> Costco.
Payless Shoe Store ==> Payless ShoeSource.
Capital Records ==> Capitol Records.
Lucasfilms ==> Lucasfilm.
Century Theaters ==> Century Theatres.
AMC Theaters ==> AMC Theatres.
Brenden Theaters ==> Brenden Theatres.
Mann's Chinese Theater ==> TCL Chinese Theatre.

Orville Redenbacher ==> Orville Redenbacher's.
Mike 'n Ike ==> Mike and Ike.
Good-n-Plenty ==> Good & Plenty.
Jujubees ==> Jujubes.
Juicy Fruits ==> Jujyfruits.
Lemonheads ==> Lemonhead.
Dum-Dums ==> Dum.Dums.
Double Bubble ==> Dubble Bubble.
Fruit Stripes Gum ==> Fruit Stripe Gum.
Cracker Jacks ==> Cracker Jack.
Funions ==> Funyuns.
Cheez-Its ==> Cheez-It.
Frito Lay's, Frito Lays ==> Frito Lay.
Lays potato chips ==> Lay's.
Tyrrel's chips ==> Tyrel's.
Tostinos ==> Totinos.
Triscuits ==> Triscuit.
Fudgesicle ==> Fudgsicle.
Twizzler ==> Twizzlers.
Red Vine ==> Red Vines.
Haribo Gummy Bears ==> Haribo Goldbears.
Kit-Kat ==> Kit Kat.
Kit-Kat, 5 pieces ==> Kit Kat, 4 pieces.
Hersheys ==> Hershey's.
Nestles ==> Nestle.
Mr. Goodbar ==> mr. Goodbar.
Ghiradelli chocolate ==> Ghirardelli.
Tolberone ==> Toblerone.
Nutty Bars ==> Nutty Buddy.
Ice Cubes ==> Ice Cube.
Uno ==> U-NO.
Rolos ==> Rolo.
Oreo's Double Stuff ==> Double Stuf.
Oreos ==> Oreo.
Pixie Stix ==> Pixy Stix.
Yorkshire Peppermint Pattie ==> Patty.
Sweet-Tarts ==> SweeTARTS.
Malteasers ==> Maltesers.

Now or Later ==> Now and Later.

Crispy Creme ==> Krispy Kreme.

Cadbury's Cream Egg ==> Cadbury's Crème Egg.

Cadbury, normal "C" ==> Swirly "C."

Eddy's Ice Cream ==> Edy's Ice Cream.

Neopolitan Ice Cream ==> Neapolitan Ice Cream.

Haagen-Daz ==> Haagen-Dazs.

Reddi Whip ==> Reddi Wip.

Coca Cola: large dash ==> Coca Cola: small, square dash.

No Coca Cola Life ==> Coca Cola Life, in green cans.

Coca Cola not sold in milk containers ==> Sold in milk containers.

Coke Zero ==> Coca Cola Zero.

Pepsi Clear ==> Crystal Pepsi.

Mountain Dew ==> Mtn Dew.

Mellow Yellow ==> Mello Yello.

(Gatorade) Quench Your Thirst ==> Thirst Quencher.

Real Lemon and Real Lime ==> ReaLemon and ReaLime.

Sunny-D ==> SunnyD.

Nesquick ==> Nesquik.

Fiji Water with palm trees on bottle ==> No palm trees on bottle.

Poland Springs ==> Poland Spring.

Juicy Juice ==> Jucee Juice.

Capri ==> Capri Sun.

Keebler's ==> Keebler.

Barnum's Animal Crackers ==> Barnum's Animals Crackers.

Captain Crunch ==> Cap'n Crunch.

Kelloggs ==> Kellogg's.

King Vitamin cereal ==> King Vitaman.

Rice Crispies ==> Rice Krispies.

Coco Crispies, Coco Krispies ==> Cocoa Krispies.

Honeycombs ==> Honeycomb.

Orowheat ==> Oroweat.

Pepperidge Farms ==> Pepperidge Farm.

Playschool ==> Playskool. (educational toys are misspelled).

Playdough ==> PlayDoh.

Mega Blocks ==> Mega Bloks.

Johnson & Johnson Baby Shampoo ==> Johnson's Baby Shampoo.

Trouble or Frustration game ==> Kimble.
Headbanz game ==> Hedbanz.
Rainbow Bright ==> Rainbow Brite.
Gordon's Fish products ==> Gorton's Fish products.
Bare Essentials ==> Bare Escentuals.
Herbal Essence ==> Herbal Essences.
Garnier Fruitis ==> Fructis.
Ultra Beauty ==> Ulta Beauty.
Pine Sol ==> Pine-Sol.
Downey ==> Downy.
Helmann's Mayonnaise ==> Hellmann's Mayonnaise.
Sketchers ==> Skechers.
Lay-Z-Boy ==> La-Z-Boy.
Elliot's Pizza ==> Ellios Pizza.
Lil Caesars ==> Little Caesars.
Quizno's ==> Quiznos.
Foldgers ==> Folgers.
Bigby Coffee ==> Biggby.
Anderson's Tea ==> Sanderson's.
Vlassic ==> Vlasic.
Bird's Eye ==> Birds Eye.
Van DeCamp's ==> Van Camp's.
Scotchguard ==> Scotchgard.
Vasoline ==> Vaseline. [Stone Temple Pilots' song: 'Vasoline'].
Noxema ==> Noxzema.
Ben-Gay ==> Bengay.
Brylcream ==> Brylcreem.
NeoCitrun ==> NeoCitran.
Fixadent ==> Fixodent.
Oral B, no line on "B" ==> Extra line on "B."
Penzoil ==> Pennzoil.
Detol antibacterial soap ==> Dettol.
Liquid-Plummer ==> Liquid-Plumr.
Fiberware ==> Farberware.
Hamilton Beech ==> Hamilton Beach.
Freedman's jewelers ==> Freidman's.
Caldwell Banker real estate ==> Coldwell Banker.
Chase logo, blue letters ==> Black letters.
Zales with normal "a" ==> Zales with odd "a."

Macy's with 1 star on logo ==> Two stars on logo.
Amazon, normal "z" ==> Curved "z."
Trader Joes, usual letters ==> Letters are in different fonts.
Office Depot, both words same font ==> Office Depot, different fonts.
Bloomingdale's, letters separate ==> The "oo" are interlinked.
Popeyes ==> Popeyes with "Louisiana Kitchen."
Ross ==> Ross, with "Dress for Less."
Osco Drugs ==> Osco Drug.
The Dollar Store, Dollar Store ==> Dollar Tree.
Ruby Tuesday's ==> Ruby Tuesday.
Applebees ==> Applebee's.
Men's Warehouse ==> Men's Wearhouse.
Haines ==> Hanes.
Draino ==> Drano.
Curaid ==> Curad.
Bandaid ==> Band-Aid.
Visine, normal bottle ==> Bottle with corner gone.
Alieve ==> Aleve.
Vick's ==> Vicks.
Vick's Vapor Rub ==> VapoRub.
NyQuill ==> Nyquil.
Epsom Salts ==> Epsom Salt.
Color Easy ==> Color Eazy.
Target logo, center red ==> Center white.
Target, larger center bullseye ==> Small center bullseye.
Nikkon ==> Nikon.
Kikoman ==> Kikkoman.
Qualcom ==> Qualcomm.
Phillips ==> Philips.
Chipotles ==> Chipotle.
Tobasco ==> Tabasco.
Scott's paper towels ==> Scott.
OdorBan ==> Odoban.
'No. 5' over 'Chanel' ==> 'Chanel' over 'No. 5.'
Rememberance perfume ==> Remembrance.
Soft & Dry ==> Soft & Dri.
LensCrafter ==> LensCrafters.
Advanced Auto Parts ==> Advance Auto Parts.

Sea World ==> SeaWorld.
Sportcenter ==> Sportscenter.
Crossman ==> Crosman.
Cannon ==> Canon.
Levi ==> Levi's.
Hillshire Farms ==> Hillshire Farm.
Western Sizzler ==> Western Sizzlin'.
Aunt Anne's pretzels ==> Auntie Anne's pretzels.
Bissel ==> Bissell.
Bare Naked granola ==> Bear Naked.
Braggs Apple Cider Vinegar ==> Bragg Apple Cider Vinegar.
MacIntosh ==> McIntosh.
Babcock Furniture ==> Badcock Furniture.
Blaine's Farm and Fleet ==> Blain's Farm and Fleet.
Buckee's ==> Buc-ee's.
Eckerds ==> Eckerd.
FAO Schwartz ==> FAO Schwarz.
KIA ==> KI [upside-down V instead of "A" & extensions].
VAIO ==> Modern-looking letters.
People Magazine letters not touching ==> 'People' letters touching.
THX logo, no extended "T" ==> With "T" extended.
Sirus XM ==> Sirius XM.
IBM Leveno ==> IBM Lenovo.
Amtrack ==> Amtrak.
U-Haul ==> Hyphen attached to "H."
Stanley Steamer ==> Stanley Steemer.
Marboro ==> Marlboro.
Tommy Copper ==> Tommie Copper.
Claires Boutique ==> Claire's.
Wedgewood porcelain china ==> Wedgwood.
St. John's Ambulance ==> St. John Ambulance.
Santa Catalina Salad Dressing ==> Catalina Dressing.
RAID, no lightning bolt ==> RAID with lightning bolt.
CVS Pharmacy logo, no hearts ==> With hearts.
Fancy Feast, no heart ==> With heart-shape.
Geico lizard, all green ==> Green with orange on head.
Raisin Bran sun with sunglasses ==> Without sunglasses.
Laughing Cow with regular earrings, nose ring ==> Cheese packs

as earrings.

Columbia Lady ==> With right knee extended.

Warner Brothers shield logo, normal ==> Shields are pointy, bottom sharper.

Chevron gas logo, red chevron on top ==> Blue chevron on top.

Spaghettios and Raviolios by Chef Boyardee ==> By Campbells.

Stouffer's StoveTop Stuffing ==> Never existed.

Coast2Coast with George Noory, normal 'A's in logo ==> Pyramids, no crossbar, upside-down 'V's.

('Scary Movie') "I see white people" ==> "I see dead people."

('Dirty Harry') "Do you feel lucky, punk?" ==> "You have to ask yourself one question: Do I feel lucky? Well, do you, punk?"

('...Wonderful Life') "Every time a bell rings, an angel gets its wings." ==> "...an angel gets his wings."

('Funny Girl') "The rain in Spain falls mainly on the plain." ==> "The rain in Spain falls mainly in the plain."

('A. in Wonderland') "A very happy un-birthday to you." ==> "A very merry un-birthday to you."

('Fantasy Island') "Boss! The plane! The plane!" ==> "The plane! The plane!"

(Burns & Allen) "Say goodnight, Gracie." "Goodnight, Gracie." ==> "Say goodnight, Gracie." "Goodnight."

"Me thinks the lady doth protest too much." ==> "The lady doth protest too much, methinks."

('3 Little Pigs') ==> "I'll huff and I'll puff and I'll blow your house down!" ==> "...I'll blow your house in!"

(Scarlett O'Hara) "Wherever shall I go? Whatever shall I do." ==> "Where shall I go? What shall I do?"

('Night Before Christmas') "...and I in my cap, had just settled down for a long winter's nap." ==> "...had just settled our brains for a long winter's nap."

('Lost Boys') "My own brother, a goddamn blood-sucking vampire." ==> "My own brother, a shit-sucking vampire."

('Stripes') "That's a fact, Jack!" ==> "That's the fact, Jack!"

('Oz') "I don't think we're in Kansas anymore." ==> "I have a feeling we're not in Kansas anymore."

('Titanic') "I'm king of the world!" ==> "I'm the king of the world!"

('Planet of the Apes') "Get your stinking paws off me you damned, dirty ape!" ==> "Take your stinking paws off me..."

('Toy Story') "There's a snake in my boot." ==> "There's a snake in my boots."

(Fred Flintstone) "Wilma! I'm home!" ==> Fred never said it.

(Ricky Ricardo) "Lucy! You got some 'splaining to do." ==> Ricky never said it.

"Me Tarzan, you Jane." ==> Tarzan never said it.

('All in the Family' theme) "...And you knew who you were then. Girls were girls and men were men..." ==> "And you knew where you were then. Girls were girls..."

(Nixon) "I am not a crook." ==> "I'm not a crook."

(commercial) "I can't believe I ate the whole thing." ==> "I can't believe I ate that whole thing."

(commercial) "...Hey, let's get Mikey! He'll eat anything. He likes it! Hey Mikey!" ==> "...Let's get Mikey! He won't eat it. He hates everything! He likes it! Hey Mikey!"

(commercial) "Nobody does it like Sara Lee." ==> "Nobody doesn't like Sara Lee."

(York Peppermint) "Get the sensation" ==> "Feel the sensation."

(Arthur Conan Doyle) "Once you eliminate the possible, whatever remains, no matter how improbable, must be the truth." ==> "Once you eliminate the impossible, whatever remains..."

(Gandalf, before falling in cave) "Run, you fools!" ==> "Fly, you fools!"

('The Warriors') "Come out to play" ==> "Come to play."

('Willy Wonka') Line not in original movie ==> Now it states: "We are the music-makers and we are the dreamers of dreams."

(Mamas and Papas, 'CA. Dreaming') "...And I begin to pray." ==> "...And I pretend to pray."

(Jewel) "Who will save your soul?" ==> "Who will save your souls?"

(Beatles, 'Walrus') "Man, you are a naughty boy, you let your hair grow long." ==> "...you let your face grow long."

(Pink Floyd) "All in all, we're just another brick in the wall." ==> "...they're just another brick in the wall..."

(Prince) "Celebrate this thing called life." ==> "Get through this thing called life."

(Prince, '1999') "Somebody's got a bomb, we could all die here today." ==> "Everybody's got a bomb. We could all die any day."

(Nilsson) "She put the lime in the coconut, and she shake it all up." ==> "She put the lime in the coconut, you drink 'em bot' up."

(U2) "I have climbed the highest mountains." ==> "I have climbed highest mountain..."

(B.J. Thomas) "Raindrops keep fallin' on my head." ==> "Raindrops are fallin' on my head."

(Eurythmics) "Sweet dreams are made of these..." ==> "...are made of this..."

(Doors) "If I were to say to you..." ==> "If I was to say to you..."

(Cars) "Who's gonna take you home tonight?" ==> "...drive you home tonight?"

(Roberta Flack) "The first time ever I kissed your lips." ==> "...I kissed your mouth."

(Deniece Williams) "Let's hear it for the boys." ==> "Let's hear it for the boy."

(Panic at the Disco) "...closing the goddamn door." ==> "...closing a goddamn door."

(Linkin Park, 'Crawling') "These walls are closing in" ==> "My walls are closing in."

(Kenny Rogers, 'Gambler') "On a cold winter's night" ==> "On a warm summer's eve."

(Aretha Franklin) 'Who's Foolin' Who?' ==> 'Who's Zoomin' Who?'

(MC Hammer) 'Can't Touch This' ==> 'U Can't Touch This.'

(Kansas) 'Carry on My Wayward Son' ==> 'Carry on Wayward Son.'

(Kansas) 'The Point of No Return' ==> 'The Point of Know Return.'

(Motley Crue) 'Theater of Pain' ==> 'Theatre of Pain.'

(Beastie Boys) 'License to Kill' ==> 'License to Ill.'

(Stones) 'Paint it Black' ==> 'Paint it, Black.'

(Pink Floyd) 'Dark Side of the Moon' ==> 'The Dark Side of the Moon.'

(Bruno Mars) 'I Wanna be a Millionaire' ==> 'I Wanna be a Billionaire.'

How to Kill a Mockingbird ==> To Kill a Mockingbird.
Portrait of Dorian Grey ==> Picture of Dorian Grey.
Crimes and Punishment ==> Crime and Punishment.
Anchors Away ==> Anchors Aweigh.
A Nun's Story ==> The Nun's Story.
A Winter's Tale, Winter's Tale ==> The Winter's Tale.
An American Tale ==> An American Tail.
The Handmaiden's Tale ==> The Handmaid's Tale.
Bridget Jones' Diary ==> Bridget Jones's Diary.
Family Man ==> The Family Man.
Goonies ==> The Goonies.
The Bee Movie ==> Bee Movie.
The Boss Baby ==> Boss Baby.
The Coneheads ==> Coneheads.
The Devil's Pass ==> Devil's Pass.
Silence of the Lambs ==> The Silence of the Lambs.
Herbie, the Love Bug ==> The Love Bug.
A Quest for Fire ==> Quest for Fire.
Pet Cemetary ==> Pet Sematary.
Gattica ==> Gattaca.
Transformers, 'Dark Side of the Moon' ==> 'Dark of the Moon.'
Superman vs. Batman ==> Superman v Batman.
Cats vs. Dogs ==> Cats and Dogs.
Meet the Millers ==> We're the Millers.
Rum Diaries ==> Rum Diary.
Don't Mess with the Zohan ==> You Don't Mess with the Zohan.
The Royal Tennenbaums ==> The Royal Tenenbaums.
Dr. Doolittle ==> Dr. Dolittle.
Independance Day ==> Independence Day.
Fellowship of the Rings ==> Fellowship of the Ring ==> The Fellowship of the Ring.
Forest Gump ==> Forrest Gump.
American Dad ==> American Dad!
Who Framed Roger Rabbit? ==> Who Framed Roger Rabbit.
Monsters Inc. ==> Monsters, Inc.
Lucky Number Seven ==> Lucky Number Slevin.
The Today Show ==> Today.
The Dave Chappelle Show, The Chappelle Show ==> Chappelle's Show.

The George Lopez Show ==> George Lopez.
The Sarah Silverman Show = The Sarah Silverman Program.
Dukes of Hazard ==> Dukes of Hazzard.
The Secret Life of an American Teenager ==> The Secret Life of the American Teenager.
Terminator, Judgement Day ==> Judgment Day.
Nightmare Before Christmas ==> The Nightmare Before Christmas.
The Nightmare Before Christmas, directed by Tim Burton ==> Directed by Henry Selick.
Coraline, directed by Tim Burton ==> Directed by Henry Selick.
(MC Hammer 'Can't Touch This') Yellow pants ==> Red pants.
R2D2 without wires on feet = R2D2 with brown wires on feet.
Original SW Stormtroopers, normal knees ==> Unsymmetrical knees: 1 square, 1 with band.
Hannibal Lector ==> Hannibal Lecter.
('Death of a Salesman') Willy Lomax ==> Willy Loman.
Will Smith in 'Men in Black,' no mustache ==> Has mustache, same with 'Independence Day.'
Freddy Krueger, red and green stripe shirt ==> Red and black stripe shirt.
('Candyman') say name 3 times ==> Say name 5 times.
('Inception') loud, foghorn blasts in movie ==> Not in movie, only in trailer.
'Karate Kid' wore red rising Sun bandanna ==> He wore black and white lotus on bandanna.
Chewbacca receives medal at end of SW4 ==> No longer gets medal.
In 'Groundhog Day,' no scene of Phil dead in morgue ==> Scene with Phil dead in morgue.
No German propaganda film in 1943 called "Titanic" ==> German 1943 film called 'Titanic.'
Only 'Golden Girls' show. ==> 'Golden Girls' and 'Golden Palace' show
Bowie's album 'Heathen,' he looked straight ==> He looks up.
Led Zeppelin '73 tour photo shows full Robert Plant in front of plane ==> Plant now blocked in famous photos by plane jet pushed way out in front of wing.
AC/DC from Austria ==> AC/DC from Australia.

Billy Corigan ==> Billy Corgan.

Deelight, Dee-light, Dee-Lite ==> Deee-Lite.

Dee Snyder ==> Dee Snider.

Creedance Clearwater Revival ==> Creedence Clearwater Revival.

Seals and Croft ==> Seals and Crofts.

Gypsy Kings ==> Gipsy Kings.

Ozzy Osborne ==> Ozzy Osbourne.

Simon and Garfunkel's Sound of Silence ==> Sounds of Silence (only on cover).

(S&G) Bridge Over Troubled Waters ==> Bridge Over Troubled Water.

(Springsteen) 'Born in the USA' with red handkerchief in back pocket of cover ==> Red cap.

Laura Ingram ==> Laura Ingraham.

The Safaris ==> The Surfaris.

Bob Segar ==> Bob Seger.

Liza Minelli ==> Liza Minnelli.

Seth MacFarland, McFarland, McFarlane ==> Seth MacFarlane.

Charles Schultz ==> Charles Schulz.

Dan Akroyd, Ackroyd ==> Dan Aykroyd.

Maria Louise Ciccone ==> Madonna Louise Ciccone.

Hilary Clinton ==> Hillary Clinton.

Barrack Obama ==> Barack Obama.

Jimmy Saville ==> Jimmy Savile.

Joel Olsteen ==> Joel Osteen.

Jason Stratham, Straitham ==> Jason Statham.

Reba McIntyre ==> Reba McEntire.

Kelsey Grammar ==> Kelsey Grammer.

Danny Devito ==> Danny DeVito.

Gary Shandling ==> Garry Shandling.

Patton Oswald ==> Patton Oswalt.

Keenan Ivory Wayans ==> Keenen Ivory Wayans.

Donald Pleasance ==> Donald Pleasence.

Chris Helmsworth ==> Chris Hemsworth.

Gordon Ramsey ==> Gordon Ramsay.

Ann Margaret ==> Ann-Margret.

Courtney Cox ==> Courteney Cox.

Darryl Hannah ==> Daryl Hannah.

Eliza Cuthbert ==> Elisha Cuthbert.
Shannon Doherty ==> Shannen Doherty
Sally Fields ==> Sally Field.
Steven Segal ==> Steven Seagal.
Wynona Ryder ==> Winona Ryder.
Lionel Ritchie ==> Lionel Richie.
John Edwards (psychic) ==> John Edward.
Norma Jean Mortenson ==> Norma Jeanne Mortenson.
Katherine Hepburn ==> Katharine Hepburn.
Jean Paul Gautier ==> Jean Paul Gaultier.
Raleigh Fingers ==> Rollie Fingers.
Danielle Steele ==> Danielle Steel.
Jane Austin ==> Jane Austen.
Edgar Allen Poe ==> Edgar Allan Poe.
Wild Bill Hickcock ==> Wild Bill Hickok.
John Merrick ==> Joseph Merrick.
Leonardo Da Vinci ==> Leonardo da Vinci.

Bam Bam ==> Bamm Bamm.
('Addams Family') Cousin It ==> Cousin Itt.
Wiley Coyote ==> Wile E. Coyote.
Calvin and Hobbs ==> Calvin and Hobbes.
Tom of Tom and Jerry with white around eyeballs ==> With yellow around eyeballs.
('Rugrats') Dill Pickles ==> Dil Pickles.
Popeye with 1 anchor tattoo on arm ==> Popeye with anchor tattoo on each arm.
Johnny Quest ==> Jonnie Quest.
Marshmallow Man, Stay Puff ==> Stay Puft.
Carman San Diego, yellow trench coat ==> Red trench coat.
Paddington Bear with yellow coat ==> Paddington Bear with blue coat.
Tony the Tiger with black nose ==> Tony with blue nose.
Disney's Pluto with red collar ==> Green collar.
Pillsbury Doughboy with blue scarf ==> Doughboy with white scarf.
Daffy Duck, black neck ==> With white ring around neck.
No Della Duck ==> Della Duck.
Sword in Stone ==> Sword in anvil.

Zero from 'Nightmare Before Christmas' with regular nose ==>
He has a Jack O' Lantern nose.
Cruella DeVille ==> Cruella De Vil.
Griffindor ==> Gryffindor.
Rodan, no horns ==> Rodan with horns.
Moral Oral ==> Moral Orel.
The Daily Planet ==> Daily Planet.
The Daily Bugle ==> Daily Bugle.
Barbie doll looked straight ahead ==> Barbie doll looks to the side.
Walter Lantz Cartoon Classics ==> Cartune Classics.
Hanna-Barbara ==> Hanna-Barbera.
Merry Melodies ==> Merrie Melodies.

Columbia ==> Colombia.
Union of Soviet Socialist Republic ==> Republics.
Marseilles ==> Marseille.
House of Hapsburg ==> House of Habsburg.
Edinborough ==> Edinburgh.
Mackinaw Island ==> Mackinsac Island.
Equador ==> Ecuador.
San Bernadino ==> San Bernardino.
Tazmania ==> Tasmania.
Ft. Meyers ==> Ft. Myers.
Macedonia, ancient country ==> Southeast European country.
Taj Mahal, big with some color ==> Smaller, all white.
No Southhampton Island in Hudson Bay ==> Southampton Island.
No Svalbard Islands ==> Svalbard Islands.
Never a "New Britain" ==> Now, there are a number of New Britains: island, cities.
Never a North Pole city in Alaska ==> City in Alaska called "North Pole."
Capital of Switzerland: Geneva ==> Bern.
Capital of Israel: Tel Aviv ==> Jerusalem.
Capital of Australia: Melbourne ==> Canberra.
Capital of Brazil: Rio de Janeiro ==> Brasilia.
Capital of Turkey: Istanbul ==> Ankara.

Cirque de Soleil ==> Cirque du Soleil.
Grand Central Station ==> Grand Central Terminal.
Smithsonian Institute ==> Smithsonian Institution.
Disney World ==> Walt Disney World.
Drug Enforcement Agency ==> Drug Enforcement Administration.
Federal Emergency Management Administration ==> Federal Emergency Management Agency.
Center for Disease, Control and Prevention ==> Centers for Disease, Control...
Guiness Book of World Records ==> Guinness.
Only Energizer Bunny ==> Also a Duracell Bunny.
'Birth of Venus,' painting by Botticelli, upright in shell ==> Venus slouched to side, almost falling out of shell.
Judge Judy with gavel ==> Without gavel.
Occam's Razor ==> Ockham's Razor.
Accupuncture ==> Acupuncture.
Anihilation ==> Annihilation.
Annointed ==> Anointed.
Diaphram ==> Diaphragm.
Fuschia ==> Fuchsia.
Hankerchief ==> Handkerchief.
Independance ==> Independence.
Licorice ==> Liquorice.
Octopi ==> Octopodes.
Qualude ==> Quaalude.
Schruncy, Skrunchy, Skruncy ==> Scunci.
Saber-Tooth Tiger ==> Saber-Tooth Cat.
Puffin bird, extinct ==> No longer extinct.
Harper Seal ==> Harp Seal.
Possom ==> Opossum.
Garbage Disposal ==> Garbage Disposer.
(faucets) Hot on right ==> Hot on left.
Yellow fire hydrants ==> Red fire hydrants.
Stop signs all red ==> Red with white outline.
Daylight Saving Time ==> Daylight Savings Time.
Thanksgiving on 3rd Thursday in November ==> 4th Thursday in November.
Haley's Comet ==> Halley's Comet.

Cupie Doll ==> Kewpie Doll.
Never a 666 cold medicine ==> There was a 666 allergy and cold relief medicine.
No Picture-Phones in the 1960s ==> Picture-Phones in the 1960s.
Christmas trees never hung upside-down ==> A history of upside-down Christmas trees.
Never a scarab-headed Egyptian god ==> Khepri now exists with 2D scarab as a head.
Never a "Lion City" underwater ruins ==> There is "Lion City" ruins in Cancun.
No Lion Airlines ==> Lion Airlines.
Never penguins in Africa ==> Penguins in Africa.
No humpback dolphins ==> Humpback dolphins.
No panda dolphins ==> Panda dolphins.
No pangolins ==> Pangolins.
No red rhinos ==> Red rhinos.
No orange alligators ==> Orange alligators.
No giant bunnies ==> Giant bunnies.
No vampire squirrels or black squirrels ==> Vampire squirrels with soft/bushy tails and black squirrels.
Rabbits, deer and other mammals were herbivores ==> Now some are eating other mammals.
No Fly Geyser or rainbow geysers ==> Fly Geyser and rainbow geysers.
Never Rainbow Trees and landscapes ==> Rainbow trees and landscapes.
No Blood Falls ==> Blood Falls.
Never trees that bled ==> Dragon Blood trees.
No red seashores ==> Red seashores.
No Boiling River ==> Boiling River.
No sun dogs ==> Sun dogs.
No Eternal Flame Falls ==> Eternal Flame Falls.
No Dark Lightning ==> Dark Lightning.
No Darvaza gas crater, "Door to Hell" ==> Gas crater, "Door to Hell."
No Peruvian Stargate ==> Peruvian Stargate.
No blue food ==> Blue food.
No black bread ==> Black bread.
Bananas from trees, right side up ==> From plants, upside-down.

No Cherimoyas ==> Cherimoyas.
No Walking Trees ==> Walking Trees.
Rocks were rocks ==> Rocks move, grow and breed.
Rainbows with blue on top, red on bottom ==> Rainbows with red on top, blue on bottom.
No noctilucen clouds ==> Noctilucen clouds.
No brinicles ==> Brinicles.
No thundersnow ==> Thundersnow.
No Nevada Triangle ==> Nevada Triangle.
No Michigan Triangle ==> Michigan Triangle.
Never a Bermuda Triangle in Alaska ==> Alaskan Triangle.
Northwest Passage, where it was ==> Located in a different place.
No full scale Parthenon in Nashville, Tennessee ==> Full scale Parthenon in Nashville.
Hawaiian state flag without Union Jack ==> With Union Jack.
Nordic flags with centered crosses ==> Nordic flags with off-center crosses.
Russian flag with hammer and sickle ==> Plus a 5-pointed star.
100 dollar bill with full blue strip ==> 100 bill with blue strip broken 3 times.
Mailmen had to deliver no matter the weather ==> They don't have to.
Always mailboxes on street ==> Mailboxes on street being quickly removed.
No 'Fallen Astronaut' sculpture left on Moon ==> 'Fallen Astronaut' sculpture on Moon.
Ben Franklin's kite/lightning experiment with key ==> With key and a bottle.
Rosa Parks was tired after work & needed to sit on bus ==> She (lighter-skinned) was already part of Woman's Movement and made a statement for women's rights.
John Smith and Pocahontas were married ==> They were never married.
William Shakespeare without earrings ==> With earrings.
King Arthur was British ==> King Arthur was Scottish.
Constantine started Christianity ==> Theodosius credited with establishing Christianity.
Eli Whitney was a white man ==> Eli Whitney was a black man.

Youngest U.S. President: JFK ==> Teddy Roosevelt.
Salem Witch Trials burned "witches" ==> They were hanged. None were burned.
No Nazi jet fighters ==> Nazis had jet fighters.
No self-driving, "autonomous" cars going back to the 1920s ==> A history of self-driving cars.
In WW2, no one died in the states ==> 5/5/45, 6 dead from Japanese bomb.
U.S. mainland never attacked in WW1 ==> Black Tom explosion, 7/30/16, by German agents.
Washington was first President ==> John Hanson could be considered and 8 others.
Jack Daniels invented by Jack Daniels ==> Invented by a slave.
Never "star-forts" ==> New and old star-forts.
Clocks with 'IV' ==> Some clocks now have 'IIII' instead of 'IV.'
Eggs, milk, cheese, yogurt are dairy products ==> They are not dairy products. Many fruits and vegetables are now "berries."
You got tetanus from rust ==> From dirt.
Meteors were mostly metallic, iron ore, etc. ==> "Most meteors are rocky in composition."
Roswell aliens were without gender ==> They were female.
Nine billion people on Earth ==> 7.4 billion people on Earth.

Nothing on the left column exists anymore! It is only the right column that exists now and *has ever existed.* How could you remember anything on the left side?

Take another look at the column on the left. Everyone who thought that was the name of the product or thing or person or quote was wrong? Nothing should be familiar with the column on the left because (in new reality) we're supposed to believe *it was always the column on the right?* People have simply gotten it wrong all this time? Bullshit. We ain't wrong for remembering how it was before the change. We shouldn't be criticized, mocked and thought of as "crazy" by New Worlders. Birdboxed, New Worlders who only see the dark universe descending and are sure: *it was always that way.* Truth is...the right column sounds *funny, odd to our ears, not how we remember.* Look it up, just as I did to find proper spelling of the products/quotes, etc. today. You'll be surprised at the differences in the new reality from what we remember of yesterday.

Packaging of familiar products have NAME-CHANGED, as the columns of jumbled memories indicate. They've also changed in very micro ways like the designs in the dots of "i"s. A dot between words when there was a dash before. Or no dash when there was one. An apostrophe added or subtracted, a bit different than it was previously. Name brands are now abbreviated, aligned with a society that texts and misspells. Many brand names have their letters suddenly *squished together.* Letters touch when they never did before. Often "A"s no longer look like "A"s, the crossbar has been removed and they're *pyramids.* Letters in familiar logos now have weird extensions or designs that we're never there before. [Not upgrades]. These little and large changes only support the idea: *They happened, virtually, overnight.*

Let's dive deeper into the mystery and possible answers: In Star Trek's Mirror Universe, explored in every series where actors got to play their evil twins...

[Episode called: "Mirror, Mirror"] Everything was a tad different, more nasty, slanted toward the Dark Side. People were mainly bad, yet had good in them. It was a negatively-charged universe of anti-matter. (We were positively-charged matter where people were mainly good and had less bad in them). They resembled us, much was the same. Only, humans in the negative world experienced a different history and turned out differently. They accepted things we'd regard as horrible and disgusting. Our principles of liberty, rights and fairness would be alien to our fascist and violent (Roman) counterparts. Remember the Federation's logo in the mirror world? A sword thrust down into a globe. If the +feds had a normal emblem, then the -feds today might have a kick-ass Warrior Woman as a symbol. Maybe we have switched places with our reflection in the Looking Glass? Maybe they found a way to do that? Star Trek/Star Wars = Predictive Programming.

My point is: The (small) product design changes, movie changes, changes in lyrics, Bible changes, etc. could simply be what is normal and always been, in that other world, the "bad" Twilight Zone universe we've warped into or has taken us over?

*On the evening of 2/21/19, I watched an episode of The Orville, which last season was Orville. At first, it was fantastic and so large of a show that I figured it was a 2-parter. Isaac, the android, who was having an affair with the doctor, suddenly shutdown. They took the robot to its home world, a cybernaut planet, that they thought wanted to join their "Union." As it turned out, Isaac was only a spy who gathered info on whether or not humans should be totally destroyed? They never wanted to join; they only wanted to judge us and then decide to terminate or not? The crew discovered underground caverns where **millions of their human Builders were piled, dead.** I was stunned and overwhelmed for a few reasons: 1) They, the insiders, dared miss-quote Sally Field's Oscar acceptance speech, but to them: was not miss-quoted and was stated in the way it's been changed. Every spoof of it, and there have been hundreds, never inserted: "Right now!" Those bastards, last night, rubbed it in America's face! That date must mark the first spoof on film of Sally's altered speech. Now, like everything else (including the Bible), we have to accept the Darkness, believe it's always been this way? 2) The show was far from original; it was the same plot as Prometheus 2. Why would the Engineers be killed off entirely by robot David or why would the Engineers seek to destroy Earth, the humans they've created? It's abominable, because God does not want to destroy its creations and we do not want to destroy God. Now killer androids with WMD are on their way to wipe out Earth! Gee, wonder what's going to happen? Ya think Isaac will have a change of heart? Instead of providing good, far-out stories anymore, with positive messages...there's much too much witchcraft, blood, red/black, Killer Women, parents killing children and children killing parents? What a world~*

Let's examine the date 'Alien: Covenant' was released. It was the summer of 2017. Mandela was in full swing by then (if intensified from late 2015). Fans of Alien were extremely disappointed [like other sci-fi franchises] that they did not receive a once promoted film called: "Paradise." It was going to provide us and the Elizabeth-character with answers on the Engineers' home world with a lot of cool shots of the big, bald guys. What happened? We were *sucker-punched again* and got "Covenant" instead, a military monster-hunt, blood and guts and no answers.

Liz was already dead and the robot committed genocide on the gods! Huh? *Madness should not be accepted.* Maybe Mandela Wave struck and "Paradise" was wiped, gone! Paradise Lost? Now there's only a twisted "Covenant" with the Devil?

This was merely one example, off the top of my head. How/why has so much literally turned to the Dark Side lately, especially since the end of 2015? THINK. Think about it and ask yourself has ANYTHING gotten *better* over the last few years? The answer might be, "No." Exactly what the Pope and Queen warned us of, a growing Darkness, a malevolent evil, that spread from "Europe." [Stay tuned]. They're not helping by warning us. They're the Darkness. What they're really doing is telling us what they've actually done to us.

(You wouldn't believe it, exactly what they're counting on).

One more personal story. For years I've ate Farmer John (was Farm John's) sausages, finger-length, 8-packs. I'm sure you've seen them. Maple-flavored was my favorite. I noticed that 99cent stores and grocery stores no longer stocked exactly what I remembered. This was months before I heard a word of the M.E. Why did they only stock "pork" sausages now? I have been waiting month after month for them to bring back or order what they had before: 8-packs, maple-flavored, that did not have the word "pork" on the packages. The pork sausages tasted all right, but not as good as the ones I knew without that word on the label. Was it merely psychological or was there really a difference in the two tastes? Maybe Mandela people are chuckling now, because they realize what has finally dawned on me: Those *un-porked* sausages are never coming back, will never be stocked on the shelves ever again! I'm stuck with the pork. Just now, I Googled the company, scanned pictures of the 8-packs. Shazam. Every one had the word "pork." What I clearly remember and sincerely waited months for...no longer exists in this reality. Damn.

~ The Mystery of the Shazam video:

What Shazam video? You mean from the supposed film people remember where Sinbad played a genie? When it was really Shaq? *There is no Shazam movie where Sinbad played a genie!*

The actor/comedian will deny it and has said:

"The movie was never real. The rumors started in 2009; I don't know where it came from. But it's not real." [answered questions from radio listeners] "It never happened." (upset) "You never saw it, and you should go to rehab..."

Of course, people could be mistaken. The "mistakes" could be shrugged off as thinking: *it was Sinbad, when it was really Shaq*. Case-closed. Then what the hell is this?

https://www.youtube.com/watch?v=tD0rchvuoMU

The YT link must be viewed by anyone interested in the Mandela Effect. This book has noted a large number of apparent "impossibilities." Here is another that will drive skeptics to the very limits on how to explain it. Let's try to explain it. The found, 2 and a half minutes of (beta/VHS) footage has to mesmerize everyone in the Mandela community. We will go through the film, step by step, because it is a major mystery (not so easily explained) and worthy of exploration.

What you will see is a clip from an old tape with some lines and strange interruptions. But this is not any type of amateur film. This is movie-quality with Sinbad as the genie, *Shazam!* That alone, destroys the idea that it was never made. The young boy and girl are actors that have been seen before in ads, TV commercials and probably other films.

The *absolute shock* for viewers is the amount of Mandelas within the 2 and a half minutes of old footage! Ten or more M.E. "coincidences"? Here's what happens:

The boy and girl go to the attic where there are boxes and other stuff around. They reminisce because mom is gone and dad must have thrown out a lot of her things.

"...There's gotta be something he's forgot in here? Something REAL, we can remember her by?" he says as he looks into one of the boxes. He pulls out a 'Curious George' book and the monkey has a tail. In today's universe, he never had one.

The girl oddly replies with a statement that directly refers to the Mandela. She says, "We have our memories. They're REAL. No one can take them from us." Unbelievable and true. Why the emphasis on real memories? As if someone is trying to *steal our memories?* Steal our past? (See film: 'The City of Lost Children,' stealing children's dreams).

There's a bizarre world map of land masses that have merged into one. Is this a suggestion of colliding worlds, everything in collision? Also, a Rubix [Rubik's] Cube is there and changes, all by itself, when an interruption occurs. This might show that it was not a continuity error, but a new world or "skin" had exchanged with the old one?

Even the next line applies: "Can you imagine if dad saw this mess?" (The change?).

The boy sneezes at the (magic) dust and *everything changes* with an interruption or flash of a TV commercial for Fruit Loops, spelled correctly, the way it was: 'Fruit.'

The children look around in wonder as if they too have noticed a big difference. There is a newspaper and we clearly read the headline: "**NELSON MANDELA DEAD**." The boy's name is 'James.' This could be a reference to the altered King James Bible? A Berentein/Berenstain book is in the scene as well as a Monopoly board, an obvious indication of the Monopoly Man's missing monocle. The list of Mandela Effects, or things changed by it, continues with the famous portrait of Henry VIII. Guess what he's holding? Not a glove.

There are a few more film glitches as if it's a bad VHS copy. Or? Are these parallel worlds that have intersected? Are we viewing Mandela-changes caught on film? An intersection of universes? Something else? Is there a reasonable explanation and not an extra-worldly one?

Suddenly a lamp appears, like an Aladdin's Lamp, that resembles a candle.

There's a Kit-Kat bar with hyphen. Amazing. Clearly seen. Sketchers and not Skechers tennis shoes. A changed map shows new Korean peninsula and curved Japan. This is reaching on my part, but the Jack O' Lantern could represent the altered human skull? What other M.E. items are we missing in the scene? There could be a few more, such as with the bicycles and "IBM"?

Sinbad, as Shazam, magically appears, performs extraordinary tricks and convinces the children he's a real genie. Later, he makes a cryptic statement: "Clint Eastwood did it, it can happen. Age ain't nothin' but a number." Does this have meaning? (Other "coincidences" do). Different dates of death? Is there a Mandela we're missing about Clint? [Later, found: from 'Dirty

Harry'].

To top it off, one more commercial flash, for only two seconds, ends the mysterious clip. I guess it's not so strange that it is another example of the Effect: A promo, TV ad appears of the cartoon: "Carman San Diego." She wears her *yellow trench coat* and not today's red one.

Astonishing! Especially when you add up all the Mandelas, gathered in this single clip, which has weirdly appeared? It supports the "nuts who should be in rehab" and blows apart those that say (including Sinbad) that the film never existed.

What are we seeing here? How can it be explained?

The cynic and Mandela debunker might say, "All right. It's Sinbad, there's no doubt about it. Someone must have gotten a copy of a film that was started, but never completed. Sinbad may be in on the scam? They could have tossed items around the attic, you foolishly believe have been *magically changed?* They haven't. Could be a publicity stunt to mess with us and the actors have to play dumb?"

That's a rational angle. But have you seen the dozen things in the 2 1/2 minutes that just happen to turn out as MAJOR MANDELAS many years later? *Nothing strange is going on?* How could the clip's makers (whatever it is?) know of a dozen Mandelas unless they were in on it? Let's assume they messed with us or it's a leaked clip of a never-completed film...

Let's say science could explain it with time-machines. What if there was a sinister purpose in the clip's creation and despicable people were behind it? Did they know the future and picked out exactly the changed items that will be noticed as Mandelas? Look how perfectly they were placed: Newspaper headline of Nelson Mandela's death? Monopoly board that faced the camera. Who keeps Henry VIII in their attic? Even the Kit-Kat bar was positioned so perfectly that you saw the freaking (missing) hyphen! Too perfect, eh?

That doesn't explain it. Why? *To 'rub our face in it' because of the power they have?*

Okay. Think. A clip was discovered that proved a Sinbad-genie movie existed. Once, somewhere, somehow. That would have been enough to prove the point. But. Did you count the Mandelas? Did it *have* to include this content, or anything

MANDELA? No. But that's all it did. It certainly should give us "food for thought."

I have no clue how this YT tape came into being, or who found it, or any of that. *There it is.* I may have been inclined to take a skeptical view, a sensible view that included rational thoughts and no magic. However. In the changed New World, I have to question and conclude: Scientific magic, magic made real, could be happening? Was there an oscillating flux going on and the *flip-flop of worlds* caught on film?

Maybe we were meant to see this, not by deceptive forces who produced it. Good forces out there? Maybe 'good guys' want us to see the Other Side or remember yesterday's reality?

C'mon! Did you view the interruptions of commercials that broke in for only a couple of seconds? *This is lightning hitting the same spot a dozen times, people!* Of all the commercials in the world to flash, it just happened to be a major Mandela (Froot Loops) and another known one (CSD trench coat)? Along with all the others in the short clip? Really? Don't you get it? Commercials! TV commercials? If not a set-up (& how could that be?) then, it appears as, in one universe...wait for it...

The Shazam movie that starred Sinbad was aired on television in its entirety! Someone recorded it on videotape off TV? Those sure were REAL TV commercials aired, with Toucan Sam who spoke. And, possibly, it was a kid's channel that would naturally air a child-oriented Shazam movie and also advertise their cartoons?

I confess: *I'd like to believe in magic.* "I want to believe." If it's right in my hand or directly in front of my face, I have no choice. How would fakers, time-travelers or Illuminati, who know of future M.E. changes, be able to piece this together, and dangle it in plain sight one more time? Not too logical. Funny, though. The less mind-boggling alternative or less-crazy answer to the mystery might be:

In one world, the full Shazam movie was made, even aired on TV...but, never made in the other world? *It could have been once produced and seen within our Old World!* That viewpoint answers why so many people actually remember seeing the movie. But. Presto, chango: Now we're suddenly in a *different universe* where it was never made [Ed McMahon-thing]? Even Sinbad insists it was never made. Truth could be that this Sinbad is telling the truth. Possibly, there's been a crossover because of Mandela~

If so, and it's worlds in collision, we're asking the wrong Sinbad. [Exactly like asking the wrong/current (-) Star Wars people about C3PO]. If we asked the other (+) Sinbad, or the lost one from the Old World, he might answer: *"What d'you mean, Shaq was the genie? It was my best performance. You need to go to rehab; that was me, man! I was the genie. Don't you remember?"*

[PS: I told a friend and his wife about the Mandela-changes and both of them have distinct memories of watching the *'Shazam' movie that starred Sinbad.* There was no doubt in their minds that when they were younger, they'd seen the whole movie. It was difficult for me to inform them of the new facts: 'Shazam' doesn't exist here on this side of the Mirror, anymore. It's been transformed into: *'Kazam,' with Shaq.* He still doesn't believe me and thinks he can find it.].

Let's look at the Mandela Effect and Stonehenge. The monoliths have changed to many people and especially Brits that know the ancient stones very well. It appears drastically different from what they remember. Stonehenge was more of a circle. Only a small section is curved now. There are extra large monoliths in center as well as small stones that poke out of the ground. These seem new to many. From early black & white photographs, one large monolith was always at an angle. Today, it has straightened to a vertical position. Some have suggested the changes in Stonehenge were due to aliens that have rearranged the massive stones. Some believe Mandela.

Investigating further, you might discover an absolutely new, curious development...

Some say, the find proves the rearranged monoliths are *not a Mandela Effect.*

I say: No. Now there are old photos of workers moving the monoliths and seemingly creating them? Way back in 1901, moving titanic monoliths, and we're supposed to believe this crap? The Stonehenge I knew was guarded and no one had ever done renovation on the stones. Stones that size couldn't be moved in the year 2001 or today! We're to believe photos of them moving the monoliths around, putting them on top other monoliths, as easy as pie, in 1901? No, no, no. This was *fake news* to lie to the public. Publicity shots for newspapers at the time. Must've been. Simple pulleys, ropes and man-power? No bloody way.

Today. If you study Stonehenge, you might find evidence of these old renovations on Stonehenge: "...do not mention, however, is the systematic rebuilding of the 4000 year old stone circle throughout the 20th Century. This is one of the dark secrets of history archaeologists don't talk about. The day they had the builders in at Stonehenge to recreate the most famous ancient monument in Britain as they thought it ought to look."

For one thing, Stonehenge was part of the ancient power grid along with the Great Pyramid, Easter Island and 10 other special grid points on the globe, 13 Cradles of Civilization. It is much older than 4000 years. Double that, would be a better estimate.

In my universe of the Old World, an 'In Search of...' episode concerned the wonders at Stonehenge, way back in the seventies. *People failed to move and raise a small 5-ton monolith with primitive means!* I've long said, "If Stonehenge was so damn simple to erect, you'd have thousands of college students erecting them on campuses around the world. Can't be done." That was the mystery. The monoliths cannot be created by modern means, certainly not by simple means...or even *moved.*

What are the old photographs of workers on Stonehenge throughout the 20th Century? Pure bull. Who says it's Stonehenge? Who says they were real monoliths? Why? Why lie to the public that they could alter the Stonehenge stones? Dark forces have always lied and deceived the masses. Possibly, to show the superiority of modern men...when that isn't the truth at all. The ancients, our ancestors, were far superior to our present "modern" technology in every way.

It could be a Mandela because this bit of old photography that shows construction at Stonehenge, never existed before. It would've been known, then. The "In Search of..." wasn't lying when they couldn't move a small monolith. It is probably the false reports of renovation "throughout the 20th Century" that is the lie and "popped" into existence in the dark world, our world now. Exactly like other Mandelas, it's news to many people.

Christ the Redeemer statue in Rio de Janeiro has also changed in appearance. It has grown in height and moved to the back of the platform complex. "Feet" have appeared that poke out of the robes, but this is something no one remembers. The famous statue is massive today and people on the platform complex below it seem like tiny ants. Yet other photographs defy that reality because they show a considerably smaller Redeemer statue. How can it be that people appear large in some photos and other photos show them much smaller when compared to it? People remember the statue positioned in the front part and not the back portion. From ground, below the mountain, probably few people noticed the *change* since a larger statue suddenly was set farther back on the platform.

The official height of the statue with pedestal is 125 feet. No way could it be only that height in today's photographs. If we measure the height of the crowds around it to 5-6 feet, then the Redeemer statue must be over 250 feet in height! This is far beyond its (new) official height and much taller than it seems in some photos: merely 50 or 60 feet in height. Does the change have meaning? *Jesus enlarged, but pushed back?*

The statue I remember was not so detailed. It was more impressionistic, a little more stylized. The face looked straight ahead, as it does in some photos where it appears smaller. But the new, big figure seems to *look down.*

A real shocker could have just happened. Is the Jesus statue in Rio de Janeiro changing daily? Only days ago, I examined photographs of the statue along with a few researcher's videos. Many items were discussed, but no one mentioned the addition on the chest. When called to my attention, moments ago, I did not remember the stone Redeemer's chest as it appears today. And I had just studied it two days earlier. The small, impressionistic statue has moved, enlarged and suddenly has become a very detailed sculpture. *Now there's an exposed chest* and lines of ribs that suggest the man's quite muscular. A heart? A heart image can be viewed in the bare part of the open chest. This is complete news to many who know the statue well and have visited it. Another addition are wounds in both hands. These recent additions are very detailed carvings and in few people's memories.

There is more strangeness and possible Mandela Effects when we examine the tallest statues of Jesus Christ on the planet. You'd think their heights wouldn't change? You'd think their heights were indisputable and would never be questioned? We are well aware of the famous Redeemer in Rio de Janeiro that has stood over the city since 1931. But what of the other JC statues? Why do they appear so unfamiliar to many people? Google 'tallest Christ statues' and you might be shocked at the images. Where have they been? Are they known to you? Some do appear familiar, but most of them seem extraordinary and utterly new. Yes, as if *they've just popped into existence.*

For example, view photos of Christ the Redeemer of Maratea. Few recall this mysterious, 69' statue of Jesus in Italy that, supposedly, has stood high above a harbor since 1965. I'm sure it *has* been there for more than 50 years, but maybe not in the Old World? Jesus appears very feminine, in a long/straight gown. Under the arms, there's almost "wings." From the top of Christ's head, protrudes an odd lightning rod that resembles a UFO saucer or Saturn! (No kidding: Satan out of Christ's head). It also faces inland, which is unusual. Most great statues look out to sea. It was supposed to be closely modeled after the Redeemer in Rio, but looks nothing like it. The Jesus of Maratea has his arms up. Another big difference is: Since when did Christ have short hair?

If you've studied the official record or records from various sources on Maratea, *you're liable to go out of your mind.* A number of good sources regard it as the "second tallest Jesus statue," after the famous one in Rio de Janeiro. Then there are references that put it at the fifth tallest Christ statue. Wikipedia: "This is the third tallest statue of Jesus in Europe, after Christ the King in Świebodzin, Poland and Cristo-Rei (*Christ the King*) in Lisbon, and the fifth in the world after Cristo de la Concordia and Christ the Redeemer..." Second? Third? Fifth? Which is it? To find the answer, let's examine maybe the best and most detailed listing of the tallest Jesus statues.

Shouldn't these be well known? The given heights are only the figure and not any type of pedestal. Also the date is the year completed. Some of these statues *couldn't have been around for that long,* yet official records tell us that they have been:

1. Christ of Peace - Bolivia - 112' - 1994
2. Christ the King - Poland - 108' - 2010

3. Christ the Most Holy - Colombia - 108' - 2015
4. Sacred Heart Jesus - Philippines - 102' - 2015
5. Divine Mercy Jesus - Philippines - 100' - 2017
6. Christ the Redeemer - Rio de Janeiro - 98.4' - 1931
7. Christ of Blessings - Indonesia - 98.4' - 2010
8. Resurrected Christ - Mexico - 98.4' - 1981
9. Christ the Redeemer of Tihuatlan - Mexico - 95' - 2007
10. Christ the Blessed One - Argentina - 92' - 1942
11. Christ the King of Almada - Portugal - 92' - 1959
12. Christ the King - Vietnam - 92' - 1993
13. Christ King of Dili - East Timor - 88.6' - 1996
14. Christ the King of Belalcazar - Colombia - 85.3' - 1954
15. Broken Christ of the Island - Mexico - 82' - ~
16. Christ the King of Les Houches - France - 82' - 1934
17. Christ the King of Los Alamos - Baja, CA./Mexico - 1999
18. Christ of Tana Toraja - Indonesia - 75' - 2015
19. Christ of the Sacred Heart - Baja, CA/Mexico - 75' - 2006
20. Christ King of Pachuca - Mexico - 75' - 1996
21. Christ King of Tupungato - Argentina - 75' - 1993
22. Christ King of the Pacific - Peru - 72' - 2011
23. Christ of Harghita - Romania - 72' - 2011
24. Christ the King - Lebanon - 72' - ~
25. Christ of the Knoll - Spain - 70' - 1931
26. Christ the King of Cali - Colombia - 69' - 1953
27. Christ King of Tenancingo - Mexico - 69' - 1985
28. **Christ the Redeemer of Maratea - Italy - 69' - 1965**

Now refer above to the oddity of the Maratea Redeemer. How could many, many references have put it second or third or even fifth? But numerous sources did. Were they simply wrong? Did they not know of the others? Maybe they didn't? The correct answer is Maratea comes in 28th! Some said second tallest? *How weird.* Did heights change, did new statues suddenly appear?

Christ the Redeemer in Rio is sixth?

How about the statues on the list that have been in existence from the '30s, '40s, '50s and remain completely unknown to most of the world? Shouldn't they be very well known, even famous? Aren't they taller than the Rio Redeemer used to be?

The extraordinary conclusion, when you tie in a wide

spectrum of Mandelas, is:

The tallest statues on Earth, the large number of Jesus statues, new ancient ruins, new islands, new technology before its time, 'Flying Saucer' Temple, the Tartary Empire with Mud-Floods and "re-sets" and many more recent surprises are all connected. They should have been known long before the last few years. *But they've ONLY been known in the last few years! It's like they just appeared.*

An incredible, ancient site is the "Temple of Jupiter" in Baalbek, Lebanon. [Don't remember it called that]. The stonework was extremely impressive and one had to ask: How did they get such phenomenal monoliths perched high upon huge stone columns? As everything has changed, some investigators have noticed that the ruins at Baalbek also appear different from what they remember.

Today, the horizontal stone blocks on top seem smaller and one solid piece. They were thicker, wider and broken, before. This is not the same ancient site. It's one thin piece across. It never was before. We should closely examine just about everything these days and see if it matches what we remember?

Let's examine the Sphinx closer. It also has changed along with other changes. Old photos and drawings show the panel on the left side of Sphinx's head was damaged and irregular in shape. Today it is not rough, but smooth. It appears similar to right panel, which is different than the way it was.

Since when was there a round opening on the top of the Sphinx's head? *People went in and out of the sculpture's head?* A room inside it that we could enter? Never before, but there is now. Suddenly, there's a complete history of it and drawings that show people who entered and exited the top of the Sphinx's head.

Old photos also show deep gashes on the front and back of the head. They are gone in the present reality. No one made repairs to the damage seen in photographs and drawings. Ruins were preserved and not rearranged or fixed in the Other World. The face appears different than what many people remember, especially the eyes. There was never a rectangular notch that almost looks like an earring under its right ear before, but it's there today. The biggest change to the Great Sphinx, apparently, is the fact that its *arms have grown*. They are much more extended than they were previously.

Gibraltar *was* an island in the Mediterranean Sea, south of Spain and north of Morocco, to many people's memories. No more. It is one more Mandela Effect that has been "magically" altered. Today, it is attached to the Spanish mainland. Exactly like every other true Mandela, a great many believe "it's always been that way," while another large group of people believe: "No, it hasn't."

Examine visual evidence from what's now called: 'Prudential Financial, Inc.,' a company that goes back to the 19th Century. We've grown up with their commercials on television and their sponsorship of programs throughout the decades. Remember their slogan: "Own a piece of the Rock"?

It took a short time to find (online) those who remembered the island of Gibraltar, in the same way I quickly found people who remembered that the Great Pyramid was once in the middle of the pyramids at Giza.

Here's one of the references:

"Many people including myself remember Gibraltar being an island near Spain and a British overseas territory. I myself never knew exactly where it was, but I knew it was an island. Many people say it was situated pretty much in-between Spain and Morocco where the Gibraltar Strait is. It is now not an island and it is literally just part of Spain at its most southern tip on the eastern side, which makes no sense because how can Britain claim a part of Spain? It would make sense if it was an island, like all other British overseas territories. Also, why is that part of the ocean called Gibraltar Strait if Gibraltar is not even the closest part of Spain to it? It is still pretty close, although many people have said it used to be right where the Strait is. I have read a few stories of people visiting Gibraltar and swearing they took the ferry to it, because it is an island. There are monkeys that are native to Gibraltar; but if Gibraltar is part of Spain, how are the monkeys not in other parts of Spain? It even looks like an island...like it just shouldn't be part of Spain."

The fellow made good points and is far from being alone.

Then there are masses of people who, of course, know differently and absolutely accept the New Reality without question. They know the history of Gibraltar, the strategic importance of "The Rock" during World War 2. View old, black and white clips or documentaries on the subject. Britain orchestrated everything at the time and built up the Rock as almost a massive *weapon* on the order of 'The Guns of Navarone.' Big guns, cannons, missiles, armaments, munitions of all types were shipped and amassed there. You'll see, **from the Spanish shore**, how Gibraltar was armed. Because it stood at the gateway or 'mouth' of the Mediterranean.

Maybe we shouldn't believe everything that's been "dropped" in front of us anymore? This is because of the "Effect" or contrary memories that have been globally perceived only in the last few years.

Consider very old advertisements and posters from Prudential Insurance. Gibraltar sure appears like an island. We don't see it from the air, or all around the Rock, to know for certain. It could be attached to the mainland? 'Gibraltar Peninsula' is an unfamiliar term.

One particular ad used the banner: "On the Lee Shore." What does that refer to? Islands. "Leeward" is an island reference and does not pertain to the mainland.

It was fascinating to look up the origin of the Prudential logo, that meant the financial institution was "solid as a Rock." What could it possibly say?

"The use of Prudential's symbol, the rock of Gibraltar, began after an advertising agent passed Laurel Hill, a volcanic neck, in Secaucus, New Jersey, on a train in the 1890s..." *[Wow. Wanna bet this has been changed information? Oh, what I would give for a Time Machine! I'd theorize: The agent passed a very solid rock that protruded out of the sea...not in Jersey].*

There are various depictions of Gibraltar, in Prudential ad campaigns and posters, more than a hundred years old. And elsewhere, in the company's offices and on the side of their large buildings. Again, sure does give the impression of one solid Rock out of the water. Why is a mountain range never represented in Prudential's ads? Ever, anywhere in their promotions, over so long of a time period? Why not show background land that's connected in the distance? If they want the *trust* of people in the world, why do they give the false impression of a lone, Gibraltar island?

The answer is known to the Mandela community, who've seen the same phenomenon happen again and again on all parts of the globe over years now: *unnatural changes.* But not to everyone. Strange. Gibraltar is not an isolated example of the Effect:

What about Costa Rica? People do not say, "Peru Island" or "Bolivia Island." But to many people, "the island nation of Costa Rica" is a familiar memory. They remember Nicaragua attached to Panama, not Costa Rica.

The Prudential "Rock" symbol has changed over a long span of time, down to the basic, stylized, simple emblem it is today. Now view a real photo of present-day Gibraltar:

Look how weird the land appears. This is reminiscent of "Laurel Hill...in Secaucus, New Jersey"? What's Jersey have to do with Spain? How do you go from one to the other? It seems as if the Rock had been "beamed" there, like something out of the 'Philadelphia Experiment.' There is no mountain range. Geographically, the Rock does not fit with the surrounding, flat terrain. I thought people "ferried" to the island? Well, you wouldn't have to if it was always attached to the mainland.

Okay. You asked for it. I have to bring out my 'big guns.' The following is such beautiful "residue" for the Mandela Effect. I love it and so will the M.E. believers. In old Popeye cartoons, after he ate spinach, he'd get strong and pump up his bicep. It often showed a 'tank' or powerful image on the muscle. I remember that once it was the Rock of Gibraltar, exactly how many remember it to be: a single, solid rock that stood up out of the sea in the mouth of the Mediterranean. It's in Google Images. Thank you, Popeye.

Since when is there a Gibraltar Island in Ohio, within Lake Erie? I've never heard of it and I went to college 20 miles south of Lake Erie. Let's assume the American Gibraltar Island has always been there. Why was a New World island named after an Old World Gibraltar? *It wouldn't be,* unless the Rock was an island.

Oh, to really have a Time Machine. My father was in the Navy during WW2, onboard a destroyer that was sunk by a kamikaze plane. Luckily, for unborn me, another ship was in the area. If he emerged from a Time Machine, one question I'd ask: "Were you ever at Gibraltar?" I have a feeling that he wouldn't say it was attached to the mainland.

Today, a new changed world and its long history are in place. We're to believe it because that's what's in front of us and what we have to deal with now. But this wasn't how it always was. Reality is a new "skin" that has been laid on top of what some people remember.

I believe every small scrap of Mandela-changes, confusion that never occurred more than 4 or 5 years ago, *connects.* From Mars changes, to Moon changes, to land changes, to pyramid changes, to history changes, to body changes, to movie changes, to music changes and even the "t" (cross) has been destroyed in ads, such as in 20*th* Century Fox, etc.

After 12/7/41, FDR stated: "A day that will live in infamy" in the old reality. This has also been changed to: "A date that will live in infamy." I think my father would agree.

~ A Case for Costa Rica Island

A fantastic learning experience happened when I found a lot of residue evidence for the island of Costa Rica, especially in the video: 'The LOST island of Costa Rica – my trip to Costa Rica." by Enrique C.

"It was early 2016, when I found out about the Mandela Effect. I couldn't believe what my eyes were seeing. It was almost like I had woken up in a new world. So many memories I held dear to me, suddenly, *wasn't true anymore...*When I was a kid, I remember my stepmother telling me she was half Costa Rican and half Colombian. I remember looking at maps, specifically for Costa Rica. There it was, an island in the middle of the Caribbean, located southeast of Mexico and southwest of Jamaica. In early 2016, I could no longer find the 'island nation' in the Caribbean. It had vanished once I became aware of this phenomenon known as the Mandela Effect. Costa Rica was suddenly a country in Central America bordered by Panama and Nicaragua. I was shocked to learn where it was now and that it touched the Pacific Ocean. It even has an island named Cocos Island in the Pacific."

Fueled by magical stories of the island his stepmother told him as a child, "Ricky" visited Costa Rica in 2018 and made the documentary in search of clues on mainland CR that it was once an island.

Some natives remembered that: "Christopher Columbus landed on a small island located by Limon in 1502 and *discovered* Costa Rica." "At the time, the island was known as 'Quiribri.' It was the first and last time Columbus visited Costa Rica..."

'Jurassic Park' was filmed on Cocos Island and was called "Isla Nublar" in the movie. *When Jurassic Park was filmed, CR was an island.*

Dean Cundy, the director of photography for Jurassic Park, said they had considered filming in Costa Rica, originally, because the story 'takes place on an island,' but Spielberg was concerned about road infrastructure and accessibility, according to an interview. The filmmakers depicted San Jose near a beach, because *it was near a beach.* Today, San Jose is nowhere near the ocean.

From the Costa Rica Star: "Why Costa Rica is Not the Best Setting for Jurassic Park." "Fact is the Jurassic period of about 190 to 135 million years ago, this country was barely an island and lacked the general material needed to bring life to dinosaurs..."

"Costa Rica was once a series of islands that were buried under a process of heavy volcanic activity..."

In Ricky's trip to CR, he'd found 'residue,' as well as anyone would if they investigated. He found two maps displayed in the video that showed CR out in the Caribbean, right where it used to be, as well as some of the best residual of South America being directly under North American and not east of it. Another, was an incredible/color drawing of the CR island with familiar cities and volcanoes. Why would CR be drawn that way if never an island? Nowhere could I find these images, but they were in his documentary.

What anyone can discover, if they dug a bit deeper, is endless references to CR as an island that go back to the 19th Century. Newspapers, books, ads, etc., that show hurricanes, volcanic eruptions or plagues on the "island" or "island nation" of Costa Rica, should be considered...*proof.* For example:

The Tobacco Plant, 3/22/1882. No. Carolina. "The earthquake that has recently devastated the island of Costa Rica, destroyed four towns and many thousands lives are reported lost."

Arkansas Gazette, 2/10/1892. Little Rock. "Several genuine

cases of yellow fever have developed on the island of Costa Rica."

Baltimore Sun, 6/4/1893. Maryland. "...Yellow fever is still prevalent at Limon, in the Island of Costa Rica."

Severance News, 3/18/1897. Kansas. "Ed C. Franklin to his parents. As this treats of his travels in the Island of Costa Rica..."

LA Times, 1900. "News has been received of a destructive storm which has swept over the island of Costa Rica last week..."

Baltimore Sun, 3/3/05. Maryland. "Ricardo Iglesias, a native of the island of Costa Rica..."

Oakland Tribune, 12/26/05. California. 'A Costa Rican Volcano' "On the island of Coast Rica is the remarkable volcano of Poas. The crater has an altitude of about 8500 feet..."

Salt Lake Tribune, 3/29/06. "The past six years, General Casemea has spent on the island of Costa Rica, where he built a railroad for the government."

Daily Tribune, 1920. Pratt Kansas. "Government of Costa Rica Recognized." By Associated Press. Washington, Aug. 2 - "The State Department announced today that the government recently set up by the Island of Costa Rica has been officially recognized by the United States."

Ohio Daily News, 8/24/20. Dayton. "On the island of Costa Rica, near Cocos Bay, the juice of a certain shellfish, which abound there, is used for dyeing."

Buffalo Enquirer, 8/30/20. NY. "'The last of the great pirates' are supposed to have buried pirate jewels and money valued at $21,000,000 on the island of Costa Rica, early in the 19th Century."

The Gazette, 9/17/28. "Caribbean Hurricane Sweeps Costa Rica Island."

Delaware News Journal, 4/4/29. "Major Glassburn told of the destruction of a plane on the island of Costa Rica which was to be used by a German agent..."

Tallahassee Democrat, 4/7/30. "Smallpox ravaging the island of Costa Rica will be attacked within 24 hours by 400 pounds of serum rushed by airmail from Philadelphia and Indianapolis."

Punxsutawney News, 12/24/30. "Costa Rica an Island."

Tampa Times, 9/2/41. Florida. 'TINY ISLAND NATION DEFIES NAZIS' "Costa Rica refuses to recall consuls from occupied territory."

Des Moines Register, 7/2/33. "Volcano of Irazu on the island of Costa Rica during recent eruption." - Associated Press.

Pottsville Republican, 7/15/49. PA. "Edwin Messinger, took for his subject the island of Costa Rica. He painted a very fine mental picture of this country, which is one of the steppingstones across the ocean from Florida to Orinoco."

(book by Steve Osman) 'Stumbling into Paradise.' "I can't wait to show them pictures of us hunting monkeys on the island of Costa Rica."

(book) 'Canadian Nursing' "The island of Costa Rica, which was never free from the plague and which held a population, few of which had escaped it..."

(book) 'Timber Trees and Forests of North Carolina.' "It is found...and into Mexico, at elevations of 6 to 8000 feet, and in the island of Costa Rica..."

Carlsbad Current-Argos, 3/15/63. "Costa Rica Island of Peace."

TV blurb for movie: 'Survival.' "Since March 1963 the peaceful island of Costa Rica has suffered the wrath of the active volcano, Irazu."

Calgary Alberta, 10/27/77. Canada. "Claude Hope on the island of Costa Rica has been breeding Coleus with spectacular results."

The Tribune, 5/15/80. Ohio. "Ellen Hogue, who was an exchange student to the island of Costa Rica..."

Asbury Park Press, 8/4/85. "Costa Rica: Island of Calm in Stormy Sea."

Edmonton Journal, 11/29/85. Canada. "Sportsmen Bobby Loud and Johnny Russell fish for tuna and dolphin on the tropical island of Costa Rica."

(book) 1989. '365 Great Stories from Modern History.' "On the island of Costa Rica, there used to live a golden toad..."

Jurassic Park, 1990. "Starting Point: The novel begins on the island of Costa Rica, (Crichton, 1990, p. 1):..."

The Tennessian, 10/31/94. Nashville. "The program was started in the U.S. by three businessmen six years ago. But its real origins are in the small island nation of Costa Rica."

(book, 1996) 'Conservatory Biology in Theory and Practice.' "The population on the island of Costa Rica was 1800 in 1975-1976 and 270 in 1985 and 1986."

CasinoSuite.com, 9/12/07. "On the island nation of Costa Rica, taxes on the lucrative online casino industry are sky-high."

GamblingSites.net. "...An online casino software provider, based in the island nation of Costa Rica."

Global Experience Blog, 3/26/08. 'Saying Goodbye to Paradise...' "You can probably tell by the title, I am soon to be leaving this beautiful island nation of Costa Rica and returning to the bitter cold of reality (and Canada)..."

The Windsor Star, contest, 8/7/09. Ontario. "Dose.ca and Alliance are giving one lucky winner a chance for a nine day, adventured-filled excursion for two to discover the beautiful island of Costa Rica complete with flights and accommodations."

Lincoln Star. Nebraska. "Brother of Leader of Island of Costa Rica is Assaulted."

Cuyaga Collection. "For many years, Costa Rica has been an island of democracy, peace and stability..."

CBSNews.com. 'World's Happiest Countries.' "The island nation of Costa Rica garnered the 14th spot on the list."

FinancialExpress.com. World News. "...Wall Street woman was killed in a tiger shark attack on the remote island of Costa Rica."

Eco-Business.com. "The island of Costa Rica generated enough renewable energy to power itself for 300 days of the year, largely through hydro-power..."

Honolulu Star Advertiser, 6/5/13. 'Sun-Island Locations.' "Sun-Island destinations: Oahu, Hawaii Island, Aruba, the Bahamas, Jamaica and Costa Rica."

During a pre-game show in 2014, ESPN's Mike Tirico stated on film: "...Cabana Beach, Rio de Janeiro, awesome scene, San Jose, Costa Rica, this nation of 4.7 million people, *island nation,* that are gathered as one..." Considerably later, Tirico had to apologize and wrote: "Oops, didn't realize said island nation about Costa Rica...know it's an isthmus..."

Tabrera.blogspot.com., 7/8/15. "The small island nation of Costa Rica has pledged to be carbon-neutral by 2021."

Televised news report stated: "Cleanup begins in Costa Rica, after a late season hurricane hits that island nation." There's no record now of CR being hit by a hurricane in 2015-16, of course. Yet the news clip exists. Look how often the term "island nation"

was used in print over the last 100 years.
THERE'S MUCH MORE.

Refer back to the boy, now grown, who was compelled to fly to Costa Rica (in new reality) to find clues to the wonderful stories his stepmother told years ago. Enrique C. sadly confessed that his stepmother (like many others) has *altered* and now believes CR as it is today, *and it has always been that way.* Ricky: "I have come to accept that I have seen a different version of her...She presently says Costa Rica has always been in Central America and was never (an island) in the Caribbean."

Ricky concluded: "It is my belief Costa Rica simultaneously exists as an island in the Caribbean, *and* a landlocked country in Central America. But for some reason, we are only able to see the version of where it is currently in Central America..."

If the news reports over a century were mistaken, such as confusing Costa Rica with Puerto Rico, then why were specific Costa Rican cities mentioned as well as the CR volcanoes of "Poas" and "Irazu"? News reports would not be consistently wrong.

Review the numerous *island* references from old newspapers, books, ads, etc., above. Why were there no reports of "Costa Rica island" or the "island nation of Costa Rica" after 2015? Surely there would have been many "miss-memories" or misprints in recent years? Why weren't they on the list? Why did the thorough investigator stop at 2015 in the new video? **This has incredible significance in regard to WHEN the big Mandela Tsunami really struck the Earth and changed the Old World into a mirrored New World~ Evidence shows it was late 2015 or the beginning of 2016.**

That's when the radical transformations happened.

Costa Rica morphed to the mainland supports the evidence that the island of Gibraltar had also merged with the mainland, and vice versa. Other global changes support the idea our planet is now very different from what it was, but only according to some people's memories.

One more example of a sudden land mass few remember is the *new continent* of Zealandia. There is an extra "continent" on

Earth now. Who is familiar with Zealandia, also called, Tazmantis? You remember being taught in Geography class that "an almost entirely submerged land mass broke away from Australia" millions of years ago? This is news to most people, but not to "5 million people," the population of Zealandia.

This is *my* theory: Mandela Wave really kicked in after 2015. That was when the Dark City Reboot distorted our bright world and replaced it with a Shadow World, a wicked replica, most of you are forced to believe because *it's right there!* Even long-standing histories of these new things seemed to have just materialized to some, but to others, *"It's always been that way."*

Critics of Mandela will oddly know the changes as real History; it was the way they were always taught in school or how they've come to know something over time. Who's right and who's wrong? There is no wrong and right in a relative argument. Both are right and both are wrong. We've been split in at least two pieces, in every way.

The theory is that all of you skeptics, Mandela debunkers, every last one of you, have forgotten the Old World and are under a negative spell. You believe this Garbage-Illusion of Reality that suddenly makes little sense and confronts us now. BUT. You cynics would have been singing a completely different tune:

FIVE YEARS AGO! It's a pretty damn/good theory. All of you that are positive...

* CR and Gibraltar were never islands. New Zealand was never one island.

* South America was always way east of North America and never under it.

* There were always two parts to the state of Michigan.

* There was always the Alpha Romeo car and never an Alpha Romero.

* Jiffy peanut butter never existed...

You who only see the New World and are blind to the Old World, do you really think Moses always had horns? *Billions of people* have been wrong over centuries because: Look! It's the "Prince James Bible," and all of you fools have gotten it wrong who've called it the "King James." Also. It's perfectly *normal and explainable* that Queen Elizabeth I or Elizabeth II is praised in the introduction of the Bible?

Really?

What would happen if, suddenly, the Old World snapped back in place?!

Yes, then, Moses would never have been associated with horns. There would be no image of God's bare ass on the Sistine ceiling. The Bible would no longer be Devil-speak. Tidy Cats returned to being Tidy Cat. Berenstain Bears changed back to Jewish. Lincoln Memorial without a fist. C3PO never had a silver leg. Darth said: "Luke." South America went west, to where it was. Continents instantly became what they were, before. Lady in the Moon shifted up and to the right of the lunar disk. The Great Pyramid switched back to center of Giza and realigned with the Sphinx. Tartary Empire, mud-floods, re-sets, giant statues, temples, strange ruins, new structures and freakish things in nature have DISAPPEARED. As bizarre as they suddenly appeared, *they were now gone!* Our dark reflection returned to the Hell spawn it came from. Like we woke up from a bad dream and everything was now wonderful, stable, better, brighter?

There would be no confusion or mistaken memories in every department, anymore. The point is you Mandela skeptics wouldn't exist, in the negative sense. You would see reality the way we saw reality and remembered. You would be taught differently in school from the way you think you were. Your Black Magic spell would be broken, your warped illusion lifted and we'd all view one, sharp, clear universe. We would only experience the Old World. Together. Un-split. Those that insisted there was only JIF, now enjoyed a nice, Jiffy peanut butter sandwich.

Why do so many people recall reality a different way, when they were never this separated or divergent before? Maybe the most important question is: **Exactly whose memories are false?** Who's under the spell and really the ones who are delusional? What does most everyone think or what does every Mandela-critic believe? They are sure the world was always as it is today in the present reality. They believe, obviously, that it's all these delusional Mandela people with the false memories. How stupid can people be? Records support the critics. Reality supports the critics. How could anyone think C3PO was all gold? *No, Moses* *was depicted with horns in many cases. It was always the PJV of the Bible and Queen Elizabeth was always thanked for her part of the English translation in the intro to the Bible.* Really? [Those views are quite mad, you know?].

At least Mandela people believe in an Old World that made some sense. The present world the critics so adamantly believe, *makes no sense.* As a man of two worlds who has researched without prejudice, I can tell critics: Your one world is wrong. You need to ("Get out of rehab") open your mind and your eyes. Maybe you'll "click" back and remember the positive world?

The people with false memories or false views are those of the great majority now that only see the illusion of what's in front of them, what the new records and new histories tell us, today. The ones who criticize the Mandela Effect. They've forgotten what was and call the Mandela community: "Mistaken."

Is the Mandela a Litmus-Test? To test if someone remembers the past, is part of the Light Side or only views and knows the new Dark Side? Remember the test in the original Blade Runner movie to see if someone was a 'replicant' or not? Why does that come to mind?

It's a great thought, that we can go from the Walking Dead...back to the land of the Living in one big flip-flop. Can we go home again? I'll keep my fingers uncrossed.

Another Mandela claim, believe it or not, is the appearance of Hitler's mustache. It now seems larger in photos, wider, bushy and angled on the ends. Rough and bushy? I remember a small strip of hair, straight, not rough or angled on ends. (Blue eyes?).

I checked Charlie Chaplin's speech at the end of 'The Great Dictator,' that mimicked the Nazi Chancellor. Supposedly, this was the first time his character spoke in talkies [now earlier Chaplin talkies?] and he wanted his Tramp-character to say something important. In 'The Great Dictator,' Charlie played a Jewish barber who, unfortunately, was a *double for Hitler.* He exchanged places with the Fuhrer. Instead of a violent hate-speech ("...Tomorrow, the world!"), Charlie said some of the most beautiful words ever put on film. Pure Socialism. If you haven't heard it, for the sake of your soul, *hear it!*

I watched the film to check mustaches, really. Yeah, I think

Chaplin's 'stash' was a tad larger than I remember. It was angled on the ends. I remember small and straight down, no angle, on both of them. Weird and different from people's memories.

If our old memories are "wrong" now, where did we get them? Of course, we truly remember that *other world* as reality. It existed in the real sense. But where did the Old World go? Where did we go? Why did things reform themselves and morph? What's doing this? Will everything eventually and unnaturally change again, even more? Fall like a 'House of Cards'? Why wasn't *everyone* caught in the new universe and totally have forgotten the old, like we've seen in sci-fi stories that dealt with Time? Or like John Murdoch in 'Dark City'? Some of us remember how it used to be and some, or most of us, do not. Is it because of all the "residue" evidence of the Old World that was not totally erased? Some see at least two universes and others insist there was never a change and it's always been the way it is today.

Is global conflict the very purpose of the Mandela Effect? WHY was it initiated? Chaos? To throw us off balance? No longer a stable "terra firma" world? A new and different way to send us to war? No more a sure and orderly planet? Have we really been split in two?

If the 'darkening' of the Earth continues, Old Worlders who remember the past are a dying breed. There will only be negative, nasty, New Worlders and a corrupted planet. Everyone would have lost the '50s, Norman Rockwell type of life, or the '60s, where *peace and love* were literally felt in the air and within people. Long ago, there was a time of innocence, a precious childlike innocence, a world that was a lot brighter and better. That's all gone now.

We've been made to forget who we were, originally, and our incredible history on Earth, long before the Mandela. Paradise Lost. Eden may never return. We'll *never* know our true history now, as a completely different past sets into place. You didn't know the fantastic stories or real history contained within the pages of the Bible, before. *You'll never know them now!*

They, the Monarchy, have insured chaos and confusion and endless wars to come. Exactly what they'd planned for centuries. I don't want to live in a world where Moses and Jesus have horns, while Hitler has big, blue, sympathetic eyes...while most say,

"Yeah, that's right."

I personally don't believe that the Mandela Wave should be taken as fearful news or anything to desperately worry about. I don't believe we've undergone a mass-extinction event like some people do. "Maybe we can use it to our advantage?" he asked, hopefully. Make our own good magic and positively control things, create a nice/loving reality? Warm and soft. Maybe we can live in our sweet dreams, and not in their nightmares? 'The Last Sith.' White Magic, white wizards. Break programming, *destroy fear!* Let's all hope and work and make a better tomorrow. We can try. Stay positive and don't go negative~

The "analysis" chapter here was going to end at this point. But. A new development has only now "popped" into reality, apparently. It's *unbelievable,* a shock to our eyes and brains and senses. What could possibly be next, the next major Mandela? What if I told you **the Titanic did not sink**? I don't mean it was switched with the RMS Olympia as an insurance scam. I MEAN: NO ONE DIED! Huh? Sure would be news if we were to discover an alternate history, where on the Titanic's maiden voyage in 1912, she did indeed strike an iceberg...*only the ship was towed to shore and no lives were lost!* Wow.

Remember the theorized new "skin" or different histories that have suddenly fallen into place? Extraordinary things, few have ever heard of, now exist? We're on the other side of the Looking Glass or certain aspects of completely different timelines have poked into our world? Today. You can actually find old, yellowed, newspapers that have reported that the *RMS Titanic did not sink!* There's not just a few. There's suddenly many real newspapers that have reported in great detail and with photos...of a completely different world, a wonderful world (in this case) where the horrible disaster did not happen. Investigate!

Asbury Park Evening Press. N.J. 4/15/12. TITANIC SURVIVES ICEBERG CRASH THO BADLY DAMAGED; PASSENGERS SAFE.

The Evening Observer. Dunkirk, NY. 4/15/12. "TITANIC" RAMMED AN ICEBERG. Largest ship ever built wrecked on maiden trip. Passengers transferred to safety.

Santa Ana Register. 4/15/12. LINER TITANIC IN TOW FOR LAND. 1300 PASSENGERS ARE NOW SAFE. Monster Ship Struck By Iceberg, Wireless Called Speedy Ocean Liners to Aid Her.

The Evening Sun. Baltimore. 4/15/12. ALL TITANIC PASSENGERS ARE SAFE; TRANSFERRED IN LIFEBOATS AT SEA. Parisian and Carpathia Take Human Cargo. Steamship Virginian Now Towing Great Disabled Liner Into Halifax. Wireless Messages State That No Lives Have Been-Lost On The Damaged Vessel.

Evening Sun. ALL SAVED FROM TITANIC AFTER COLLISON.

Dramatic Telegrams of Disaster. **Every man, woman and child on the great liner is safe**. "It would appear that once again the value to humanity of wireless telegraphy has been established, for at least 5 vessels are known to have hastened to the aid of the world's greatest ship when she flashed forth her appeal for help."

The Vancouver – Last Edition. TITANIC SINKING, BUT PROBABLY NO LIVES WILL BE LOST. Greatest Ship In The World Hit Iceberg Last Night – Was Badly Damaged And Now In Sinking Condition. Desperate Effort Being Made By Steamers Having Her in Tow To Beach Her On Newfoundland Coast.

Oakland Tribune. 4/15/12. TITANIC SINKING. Passengers Saved. Limping Toward Halifax After All Aboard Are Rescued.

TITANIC'S PASSENGERS SAVED. Liner Being Towed To Halifax. Caption: "View of Disabled Liner Showing Where Great Iceberg Probably Crushed Her Hull." (The photo was a stock-photo of the Titanic and its bow section with dotted lines that represented the front dent from a frontal collision. That's not where the damage was in my (our) world: the liner was cut from the side and gutted like a fish with a long gash).

The World. N.Y. -Monday. 4/15/12. TITANIC IS REPORTED SINKING. Giant Bow Of The Titanic Crumpled After Collision With Iceberg. Disabled Ship Under Tow. Passengers Including Many Notables Are Transferred To Carpathia and Parisian.

World's Biggest Ship Reported in Bad Shape After Collision At Night And Now Being Towed To Halifax By The Allen Liner Virginian.

Passengers Transferred To Cunard Liner Carpathia – All Are Now Safe.

New York, Monday. Twenty Special Trains For The Titanic Passengers. Passengers Are Expected To Reach Halifax To-Morrow. "The Titanic's passengers are all saved and are expected to arrive at Halifax on board the Baltic some time on Wednesday. The Titanic herself has sunk." [All the towed-Titanic, newspaper reports are consistent, except for this one that stated it *sunk*. Could the ship have sunk near the end of the tow, as it "limped" to shore? White Star officials may have covered up this small detail in the newspapers and maintained its "unsinkable" motto (in the other world)].

Passengers Safely Moved And Steamer Titanic Taken In Tow. Bulkheads Hold. Company confident steamer is unsinkable and will float until Halifax is reached.

"No lives in danger." Mr. Franklin, vice-president of the White Star Company (still) states that the Titanic is "unsinkable."

"...Only the Titanic's water-tight bulkheads prevented the most appalling disaster of modern times...The Virginian, the Parisian and the Carpathia, catching the wireless appeals for help, all seem to have arrived beside the Titanic about the same time this morning."

The Detroit News. 4/15/12. TITANIC'S 1,470 TAKEN OFF IN MID-OCEAN WITHOUT LOSS OF A LIFE. Wireless again averts disaster, summoning help.

The Daily Mirror. 4/16/12. TITANIC WITH 2300 ABOARD IN PERIL. EVERYONE SAFE. PASSENGERS TAKEN OFF. Helpless Giant Being Towed To Port By Allan Liner.

THERE'S MUCH MORE.

Doh! Seriously? Yes. You'll find these Google Images right alongside papers that report the ship sunk, hundreds of lives lost, you know, like the movies? Like the history we're all familiar with? The movies didn't get it wrong, but it also didn't get it quite right. Because, like everything, the world seems to be split now or fragmented. I know these [not phony] old newspapers are from a different timeline that never existed previously.

Do you recognize a pattern?

There's even photos in the newspapers of a saved Titanic. It's being towed by a strong liner called the Virginian, used as a "tugboat."

The closest ship, the Carpathia, is familiar in the saga of the Titanic. But the Parisian? That's new.

I happen to be obsessed with the Titanic, seen all the movies [new German propaganda 'Titanic' film made in 1943?] and years ago have done computer searches. I also believe *I was on the ship in a passed life* (can't swim), which would explain my obsession. I've read many newspapers on the disaster. But that was long ago, before the Mandela Effect and before so many brand new things "popped" into our world.

Old reports of a saved Titanic *never existed before!* Now they do. Of course the Titanic sunk and was never towed to shore! But that's only in one reality. Here's another timeline, with a different set of circumstances, that's 'pouring into our world'? Look at the consistencies in the reports: 'Virginian, Allan liner, towed a front-crumpled Titanic to Halifax, everyone saved.' There could be more of these types of newspapers in time.

Are you so sure Nelson Mandela didn't die in prison? Maybe in the Other World, he did? *This is like JFK not killed in Dallas or Hitler murdered in the '30s.*

The old newspapers that repeatedly stated: "The island nation of Costa Rica" were echoes of the Old/Lost World. The above newspapers, with photos, could also be real. The difference is a "Saved Titanic" is from a completely different universe, which we unanimously agree upon, of course (I think).

The Titanic was an elaborate murder plot to kill the opponents of the Federal Reserve: Astor, Guggenheim and Straus. A war between bad rich guys and maybe the last 3 decent, rich guys? The wealthiest people were highly courted onboard the maiden voyage of the "unsinkable" ship. If you were of any high class, you were coaxed to be in First Class on the Titanic. The three had to have been murdered by assassins, as the plan was all along. Some men were saved and certainly these incredibly wealthy men would have been the very first saved. They were probably killed.

What happened in the other world where the liner was towed to safety and Astor, Guggenheim and Straus survived? What happened in that 20th Century, possibly, without a Federal Reserve? Look at the intense trauma to the psyche that would not have occurred?

From 'A Night to Remember': "...Because even though it's happened, it's still unbelievable. I don't think I'll ever feel sure again...about anything."

What of many hundreds of people that did not perish in the disaster? Families, generations of people, that would never have existed if history flowed a different way?

Isn't it wonderful to believe? Such a beautiful dream, eh? To think that every newspaper and many more unseen belong to a real universe where the *Titanic didn't sink and everyone was saved~* Wow. Imagine that bright, clear, April morning came and there wasn't a mass of frozen, dead bodies in the ocean. Every soul was saved and it was a glorious morning.

**** *Why is M.E. happening? When did it start and who is responsible?*

What was the date of the Mandela Wave? When did the changes first happen? When did my mother's King James Bible turn into the *Prince James Bible* and into 'Devil-Speak'? These are very important questions. Possibly, they can be correctly answered if we examined the clues? For example:

Remember what the Pope said to the masses in St. Petersburg Square at the end of **2015**? Pope Francis stated that: "End times were coming" and by this time next year (Christmas, 2016), it will be nothing like we've ever seen before. He warned us of a coming "World War 3." The Pope said that this: *"Could be the last Christmas."*

Remember Queen Elizabeth's Christmas message in **2015**? Since the beginning of television and earlier on radio, she has always addressed countries in her empire at Christmas time. Millions of people remember her grim, creepy statement for us to: "**...Enjoy your last Christmas**." She spoke of light and dark, that an *evil malevolence has spread across Europe and takes hold more and more every day.* This was aired right after Pope Francis addressed the masses and said the exact same thing.

Reports say Elizabeth confessed to the murder of Princess Diana in the first take for the BBC. It was redone and the audience never heard a full confession of the Monarchy's sins. A Mandela Effect may have occurred because you cannot find the film, the tape, or any broadcast version of the Queen saying: "Enjoy your last Christmas." I tried to find the film and quote what she said exactly. No. Can't be found. You can find the same 2015 Christmas address, same clothes, same setting, but there is no mention of "Last Christmas." Gone. Millions didn't hear wrong.

A few had noticed that it didn't appear like it was the same Queen in the redone broadcast. Could there have been a switch of polarity? Was there the last shred of a positive Queen that was about to confess to a multitude of horrors (because her time was running out), then polarities switched, even physically, and she transformed back into the Wicked Witch, again?

It's very odd you cannot find her "Doomsday Christmas" statement, yet millions heard it, reported it, talked about it and clearly remembered it. Here was one quote out of many thousands online: "She did. I saw it...But now...It's GONE! Mandela effect. Not a game. Not fake news...We all saw it, we all heard it, but no..."

What does it mean? What do the Pope and Queen's statements suggest? Possibly. What if these monsters and printers of Money and movers of the world had found a method to open a doorway into another world, back in 2015? To switch and change places and become our evil, mirror counterparts? Could it be that 2015 was the last time our planet Earth was real? Maybe that's when the Mandela-transporter-wave really struck with full force *and fucking changed everything into their dark image?*

When did physical things really start morphing? When did someone first notice that the Berenstein Bears turned into the Berenstain Bears? And Jiffy went to JIF, etc.? When did your friends and family suddenly start acting like your enemies? [Could be just me]. These incredible, physical changes started occurring right after the Pope and Queen's speech. Didn't they? *Those bastards.*

Connect that with the impossibility that that BITCH on the throne found a way to insert herself and praised her fucking self over and over again in the James introduction of the Bible! How the hell did she manage that? Black, evil, negative Magic! A push of a button, a pull of a lever, a turn of a dial...

And Harry Potter wizardry becomes true~ *Hazaaa! Shazam! Abracadabra!* It's now real and they can manipulate the Earthly Holodec parameters, the virtual reality that now surrounds us, any way they desire? Masters of the Universe. Or they found a negatively-charged universe of antimatter and was able to exchange places with our dark, twin reflection? "Magic Mirror" or "Looking Glass."

I had written the following paragraph previously, when I first wondered: WHY would the super rich elites do this?

Purpose: to completely change the landscape to evil and

wrong, backward behaviors. A modern means to stay in power. Modern magicians found a mechanical way to do it and warp our real world into a negative facsimile of it that THEY control and manipulate. In past, they've been highly skilled at brainwashing our minds by multiple Media techniques of Mind Control and traumatic "Psy-Ops." Now they've actually discovered a way to move or rearrange our physical world so we'd argue about the chaotic menagerie around us and would hardly believe the insanity.

They shouldn't get away with it! I'm mad as hell!

~ How is it possible for them to make Harry Potter wizardry in the real world? How could the Mandela Effect happen?

The question can be correctly answered when we consider two points:

1) **Humanity, technologically, is far more advanced than what we realize**.

2) **They're not going to share knowledge and technology with us**. Never have.

Do we know and use Tesla Technology? Of course, we don't. For 120 years, they've hidden Wireless Electricity based on radio-induction principles from us, and kept it for themselves. And so much more: water-engines, free-energy motors, etc. Quantum leaps of innovation have not happened for us, but have for them. Know of "Time Machines and Particle-Beams"? (Should be a song). They've been around for a half a century. Researchers who dig into what they've hidden from us, will discover that TIME MACHINES and other fantastic things are real! Study the 'Philadelphia Experiment,' started by Tesla during WWII, if you want to understand a little of what's been sealed away from us.

There is certainly a "they" and "us." Look to the dollar and a distorted (wrong angle) Egyptian pyramid. It is the kingly and queenly rich bloodlines in the very top capstone that see themselves as holy, divine. They think they are "the illuminated," fated to rule, and are symbolized by the one eye [not God] with rays of enlightenment surrounding it. The dollar eye-image has been used to represent "Big Brother" in George Orwell's '1984,' which today could be called: *"Big Sista."*

There is a space below the capstone and then there is the rest of us. The most famous people on Earth and some of the most wealthy are in that top/lower tier, but can never enter the highest levels of "royalty" above. Stanley ('2001') Kubrick couldn't get in and he served them well.

"They" print the money and "we" are enslaved by it. "Annuit coeptis" means: "Our Enterprise has been crowned with success." In other words, the secret/fascist Zionist plot to take total control of the Earth...via world money (throne of England), world religion (Vatican) and world military (Pentagon). It has succeeded.

In the lower levels of humanity's pyramid on the dollar, poor people are represented down to the very poorest at the bottom.

One more time, movies/films/fiction will be suggested as "Predictive Programming," where THEY [British Gate-Keepers, controllers] keep us controlled by Media and also tell us of actual things they're planning or have done...in movies. Exactly like how Nazis used Media for propaganda, and *pushed agendas.*

Classic **Science-fiction is not fantasy**. Sci-fi has always shown us 'Things to Come.' Sci-fi is what humanity will achieve in the future; we just don't have this technology yet. But we will in time. (If allowed?) Let's review a few films:

In H.G. Wells' 'The Shape of Things to Come' and film with Raymond Massey, humanity was caught in a seemingly endless World War that lasted throughout the 20th Century. *But by the end of the century, war was no more.* People worked together and built a utopia. Their children were brilliant and were sent to the stars!

The 1930 film called 'Just Imagine' starred Maureen O'Sullivan. It projected what the world would be like only 50 years into the future. (Not fantasy) Their views of the Earth in 1980 would *astound you* and were similar to Huxley's 'Brave New World.' People were born as "Test Tube babies." They flew in saucer-type vehicles, much like George Jetson. *It was 1980!*

How about 'Space 1999'? Maybe some global 'federation' have had bases on the Moon for decades, but not the general public. Do you realize how long we citizens of Earth have been (lied to) promised trips to the Moon, space-bus tours to safe habitats on the lunar surface? For more than 60 years! They'll *never* let us get there. Look what happened to the "first civilian in space"? It's for them, the royalty and special elites in the *'capstone.'* Not for us. They have moonbases and probably Mars bases, we don't. They don't share.

The federal 'Aurora' spaceship had made regular trips to the Moon and into space for decades, so legends say. Possibly, many other secreted crafts could've even traveled to other planets by now at light-speed? *Teleporters? Stargates? Time-Tunnels? Wormholes?* But we commoners aren't a part of that dark cabal at the top of things, are we?

Mandela Effect

If you put '1964 Visions of 2011' in Google, you'll come to my article, something I had to write when the spirit moved me back in 2011. I watched an old 'Outer Limits' episode from 1964 that I've surely seen a few times before. The oddity was it concerned or projected 47 years into the future: the year of 2011. Huh? *Since it was 2011,* the differences of what they thought would be the future, from what was the present, would be very interesting. *What a difference!* We'd explored deep space. We collected so many specimens of lifeforms from various planets, we had alien zoos for the public. People lived in fantastic homes, domes or disk-shaped dwellings raised on giant poles we've seen on the 'Jetsons.' [No special-effects, they filmed at a real futuristic home in 1964, raised atop a big pole]. Media, communications, weapons and vehicles were all far more advanced than even today in 2019.

What happened? Why no jet-cars, jet-packs, hovercrafts, moving-sidewalks or trips to Mars?

Remember the film: 'Elysium'? Not only were the elites off-world, they had CURES and high-technology for them only, while we suffered upon a dying planet. They have the advanced technology; they simply won't give it to everyone.

Films like '2001' and '2010' and a heck of a lot more had forecast vast innovations and near 'miracles' by the 21st Century.

Do you know what time it is?

Most people are led to think in a solid, unified HUMANITY, one world, *not in a split society with a few corrupt leaders ruling everyone else under the Iron Fist of lies and deception.* There has not been one people for thousands of years. Under kings and queens, there has only been the rich and the poor. 'We' will never receive what 'they' have, had and will have access to.

There is no Democracy. There is only the State, the "Republic," (look up definition) which is a rule "by council." In other words, everyone is under the Supreme Authority of a small group of dictators, aka secret societies. "I pledge allegiance to the United States, and to the REPUBLIC..." Like Republic of China? It should have said "democracy."

Have you seen the "fasces" (fascist) symbols on the walls in the House of Representatives and the crossed-fasces on the round Senate seal? Or the symbol on the back of the old Mercury dime?

They originated from Roman times. It means: "If you control the leaders through Freemasonry (tied rods), then you have power (ax-head)."

Today, THEY, a few on top, fly through space in disks like George Jetson, while we grovel in bedrock like Fred Flintstone. Buck Rogers and Flash Gordon-stuff are for THEM and not for us. They keep science, technology, knowledge, history and the truth from us.

So...you think they *wouldn't* hide the good tech from everyone? Think again. They certainly don't want us smart. They probably have 'Sherlock,' while we're stuck with stupid 'Watson.' We pay for it with our taxes, but we all do not share in the fruits of that wondrous, super technology. Do we? What amazing 'magic' they can produce when they are completely in charge of printing the planet's money! They go through Time; they smash atoms in CERN Colliders; they control global weather; they beam via teleporters (no flies) and replicate foods and other materials, etc. They also have really opened portals to other dimensions, other universes. Parallel, and a lot more. This has not been done for good purposes that benefit us. It's been done to benefit the 'royals,' the few on top. How much of the movie 'Men in Black' is real?

They never do the right thing with super technology, do they? The Good Magic? Magnificent things for us: "on Earth," do they? There's never been good news on the news, *not really.* They make sure of that. They never implement positive technology into society, scientific wonders that benefit everyone on the planet, do they? Nikola Tesla would have, if he was permitted, 120 years ago.

How can this be true, said or believed? Possibly, maybe, because every other film released is now *wicked!* Have there been and are there hints in movies? They open a portal to another world and it's always HELL! Disney's 'The Black Hole' or 'Event Horizon.' The 'portal' is in a haunted house or your house or in the woods. Johnny or Meghan are possessed...but, they're never possessed by good spirits, are they? Always bad, fallen angels and never loving angels. Never something positive. Never good aliens, always bad aliens, killer aliens. Wicked Witch and never Glinda. Never a passage to a Good Place with nice, sweet things, fuzzy, soft and warm, eh? TV show 'The Good Place,' turned out to be the Bad Place. Yeah, *it was Hell.* Another example is Netflix'

'Stranger Things.' They, of course, open a portal to an evil, dark, parallel world. It's called: "The Upside-Down." No surprise. Why same story over and over again? Maybe they've been telling us what they've planned and done for a long time now?

What was the plot in 'The Matrix' and what was the real world? Our reality was not real, but a synthetic fabrication. It was a completely different year in the future, a dark/dangerous/twisted world and there was a war with the machines.

Other works of fiction have been associated with the Mandela Effect: 'They Live,' 'Jacob's Ladder,' 'Groundhog Day,' 'TRON,' 'Dark City,' 'The Thirteenth Floor,' 'The Dark Tower,' 'Upside-Down' and the show 'Lost.'

View George Orwell's 'Nineteen Eighty-Four' on YouTube. View both black & white versions, filmed long before the colored one with Richard Burton and John Hurt. The English film from 1954 starred Peter Cushing (once played Lord Tarkin) and the American version of '1984' in 1956 starred Edmond O'Brien. Like H.G. Wells' TTC story, the planet was locked into an eternal War. Orwell told us who is to blame. '1984' told us who is to blame. Who were the terrorists, who bombed the good people? [Who ordered the attack on Pearl Harbor, 9/11 and the London Blitz upon *only poor people?*]. Who does Winston discover is behind the endless War? ENGLAND, Big Brother, the STATE! **There is no Enemy. The true Enemy is Big Brother, the fascist State that we all serve**. What's Orwell trying to say in his masterwork that is not fiction?

'1984' IS A WARNING OF WHO IS IN CHARGE OF THE WORLD, WHO CAUSES ALL WARS AND IS BEHIND ALL TERRORIST ATTACKS: **The Monarchy**. The Vatican. The Pentagon. The Throne of England. The New Roman Empire. The York that controls New York. New World Order to even *a newer World Order.*

The few on top have power. The many on bottom do not.

The war has been over, long ago.

We lost.

BRITAIN IS DIRECTED TO PUSH BUTTONS, PULL LEVERS, TURN DIALS AND BRING MORE AND MORE NEGATIVE FORCES INTO OUR EARTH, ONTO OUR

PLANET, FROM OUTSIDE/EVIL DIMENSIONS. WE SHOULD KNOW THIS BECAUSE THEY HAVE TOLD US OF THE **BLACK MAGIC** THEY HAVE CONDUCTED OVER AND OVER AGAIN IN STORIES FOR A LONG TIME. THEY LAUGH AT US FOR OUR STUPIDITY [THEY'VE CREATED] AND BECAUSE OF THE POWER THEY WIELD OVER US. THEY CAN AND WILL DO JUST ABOUT ANYTHING. WE CANNOT.

Hugh Everett III (1930-1982) was an American physicist who first proposed the "many-worlds" interpretation of quantum physics. He was "discouraged by the scorn of other physicists" for his *Many-Worlds Interpretation*. The hypothesis states that there are an infinite number of possibilities or realities created by every single decision we make. When we come to any fork in the road and make a decision, a certain set of consequences are the result of that action. But the alternate decisions, roads not taken, also create parallel universes and different consequences, different realities. Alternate worlds of alternate decisions also exist? Fascinating.

Everett's controversial work is only mentioned here to inform you that mega-worlds, the Mega-verse, multiple universes, what String-Theory and quantum mechanics will tell you is there is NOT ONE WORLD. It's infinite. This might apply to the Mandela Wave, which could have bridged the gap between parallel worlds.

A word about the Flat-Earth. No one was a bigger opponent than Tray "Galileo" Caladan! Do you people have flat heads to think that? Have they made you so stupid and really pushed you back to Feudal times, when you should be centuries ahead of where you are? Success! You've become the dolts they want you to be. Then, (same as skeptical of Mandela, initially) as I realized [DAMN!] Mandela was true, there were too many changes to what was, now...

If our entire world, not just Earth, is or has become an artificial, photonic construct and we could be digital data, 1s and 0s, on someone's computer screen?

Therefore, it's not a matter of a "Flat-Earth," anymore. **It's a Flat-Universe!**

Maybe?

~ Finally. Accepting the reality of a transformed Old World into a different universe, like a bad 'Reboot' game has fallen upon us and taken over, even *wiping memories,* it might be asked: "What can we do? Play the game out? Pray to the angels? Pray to the aliens? Where do we go? What can we do?"

I've been praying to the aliens since my contact in 1973, look where it landed me. I'm not in limbo. I'm not in purgatory. I sure ain't in Heaven. *There's only one more!*

I really have Prayed to the Aliens, I'll bet a lot more than Gary Numan. Until very recently, still imagined a gigantic saucer of peaceful Space Brothers coming to our rescue, coming to fix things, putting things right. It would not turn sinister like 'V,' 'Independence Day' or *"It's a cookbook!"* The contact would be real, true and good, like a Care Package from the Enterprise.

But lately, I've thought differently: If we have been virtually beamed into a TRON game, and losing badly, we need TRON. If we're actually in a holodec of someone's VR program...then there might not be a big/bright universe filled with life around us, anymore. Stars once were endless solar systems. *Alien and advanced human life were everywhere! (They didn't tell you).* Today, in the fluid environment that surrounds us, I'm not sure what suns are anymore. The whole question of life out there and any kind of contact or help from them might not be possible?

I'm dreaming, praying, still...for a way out of madness, for a way to go back home to a bright, positive Old World. Polarities to switch again? Maybe what we really need are Computer Programmers, outside Visitors, good *users* that are working on the problem?

"Hey! We're in here, get us out of the darkness!"

Yes, it's wishful thinking. Someone out there that knows how much we've been screwed with and are doing their best to get us solid, stable and real again, without any collisions from parallel worlds, to "clean up the mess"? Wow. That would be beautiful. A huge spaceship would probably not appear in the sky, then. It might appear more like a 3D rift or a computer matrix-port in the sky, rather than any type of vehicle?

I like to keep positive: a light in the Darkness, and all that...

TS Caladan

☯ PREDICTIVE PROGRAMMING

"I don't think the Sun even exists, in this place...damn right, *this is crazy*...It's not just me, it's all of us. They're doing something to all of us..."

(stops car) "I don't understand. There used to be a bridge here."

"They abducted us and brought us here...it's their experiment. They mix and match our memories, as they see fit, trying to define what makes us unique."

"Why are they doing all this?"

"...It is our capability for individuality, our souls, that makes us different from them. They think they can find the human soul if they can understand how our memories work. All they have are collective memories [Borg]. They share one Group Mind. They're dying, you see? Their race is on the brink of extinction. They think we can help them..."

"TUNE...They have machines buried deep beneath the surface that allow them to focus their telepathic energies. They control everything here....(They) remix it, like so much paint. Give us back new memories of their choosing..."

"...You were never a boy, not in this place (Shell Beach). Your history is an illusion, a fabrication, as it is with all of us..."

"...None of us remember that (Old World, is)...*somewhere else...*"   ~ 'Dark City' (1998)

The simulation inside the simulation said, "It was true. It was all a sham. It ain't real...I wanna know: why? Why would you put us through this? *Why ya fucking with our minds?!"*

Doug Hall replied, "You weren't supposed to find out..."

"Well I did. And now I want you to show me...what is real?"

~ On the other side, in the "real world" that wasn't...

"...He tried to kill me...He (avatar) found out his world isn't real. This is a mistake. The whole project, this experiment! *We are screwing with people's lives!"* Hall screamed at his programmer friend.

"You're talking crazy..."

"These people (in VR program) are *real*. They are as real as you and me."

"Yeah. That's because we designed them that way, Doug. But in the end, they're just a bunch of electronic circuits....You can't just pull the plug and go home!"

"I know the truth." [programmer Doug realized his "real world" was fake].

"Where are you?" she asked.

"You can call it the 'End of the World.'"

"How many simulated worlds are there?" he asked her.

"Thousands. But yours is the only one that's created a simulation, inside a simulation. Something we never could have expected...We programmed this world so no one in it could ever learn the truth..."

"There's only one flaw...none of this is real. You pull the plug...I disappear," Doug told her.

Simulation, on the other side, said, "What did you do to the (my) world?"

Doug responded, "Turned it off."

He was frightened and yelled: "Well, turn it back!"

"I'm just like you. Just a bunch of electricity."

"What are you talking about?"

"It's all smoke and mirrors. Just like your world, we're nothing but a simulation on some computer..."

"What?" the confused man from a 1937 program asked.

"It's like a machine...(We're) all following pre-programmed movements, generated by electrical energy."

"What are you saying? There's another world on top of this one?"

"That's it."

Cop said to the girl: "When you get back to wherever it is you come from...just leave us all the hell alone down here, Okay?"

~ 'The Thirteenth Floor' (1999)

Flynn said: "Our worlds are more connected than anyone knows...*Game over*...Clu's planning something, we've known that for awhile. ["Purge"]. Programs have been disappearing; there's unrest out there. Even revolution...it's his game now. [The Dark Grid]...The only way to win is not play. This is all his design: to change the Game..."

"...A digital frontier to reshape the human condition..."

"I always thought that was a plot line," Sam replied.

"In our world, she (iso) can change everything..."

"What's it like, Sam?" Quorra asked.

"The Sun? Man, I've never had to describe it before. Warm, radiant, beautiful..."

(Clu, to large crowd of minions) "At this moment, the Key to the next frontier is finally in our possession! I will make the world OPEN, and available to all of us! All of us! There, our system will grow, our system will blossom!"

"He's figured out how to do it," Flynn gasped.

(In the real world) "What's next, Sam?" Quorra asked.

"I guess...we're supposed to change the world."

~ 'Tron: Legacy' (2010)

"In a world where the laws of physics do not operate, there is no reality...The bullets are not real. Phantoms! Ghosts. They are to be ignored..."   ~ Mr. Spock, 'Spectre of the Gun' (1968)

"I think, therefore I am."   ~ Rene Decartes

"You have the look of a man who accepts what he sees because he's expecting to wake up. Ironically, this is not far from the truth. Do you believe in fate, Neo?" Morpheus asked.

"No."

"Why not?"

"I don't like the idea that I'm not in control of my life."

"I know exactly what you mean." (sits) [**MISSING LINE**]. "...Let me tell you why you're here. You're here because you know something. What you know, you can't explain. But you feel it. You felt it your entire life. *There's something wrong with the world.* You don't know what, but it is there. Like a splinter in your mind...driving you mad. It is this feeling that has brought you to me. Do you know what I'm talking about?"

"The Matrix?"

"Do you want to know...what it is? The Matrix is everywhere.

It is all around us. Even now, in this very room. You can see it when you look out your window...or when you turn on your television. You can feel it when you go to work...when you go to church...when you pay your taxes. It is the world that has been pulled over your eyes to blind you from the truth."

"What truth?" Neo asked.

"That you are a slave, Neo. Like everyone else, you were born into bondage, born into a prison that you cannot smell or taste or touch. A prison for your mind."　　　　　~ 'The Matrix' (1999)

Roland, the last Gunslinger, said to the boy: "...The ancient structures are before [after] the world moved on. Who knows what they are?...It was our final stand..."

Jake asked, "Was it about the Tower? The war?"

"Yes."

(Walter, Man in Black, commands two henchmen) "Now KILL...*each other.* (to crowd) Calm down. Enjoy the show, folks. You ain't seen nothin' yet."

Roland told Jake: "It's a map. [Tartary north pole map?] My father showed me. Inside the circle, is your world and mine, and many others. No one knows how many. The Dark Tower [pole rock] stands in the center of all things. And it's stood there from the beginning of Time. It sends out powerful energy, protects the universe, shields us from what's outside..."

The boy wondered, "What do you mean? What's outside the universe?"

The Gunslinger told him, "Outside is endless Darkness, full of demons trying to get to us. Walter (Man in Black) wants to tear down the Tower and let them in. When the Tower falls, he'll rule, in a world full of monsters...What happens in one world, echoes in others...That was just a small tear. They happen after every attack on the Tower."

In the other universe, Walter declared, "The boy is quite special...He's here on Mid-World." (boy is captured) "Your gift is extraordinary, Jake. It made you see across worlds."

Later, Roland told the boy: "The Man in Black and his men,

keep track of all portal travel..."

"Portals?"

The Gunslinger ordered: "You're going to send me to Keystone Earth."

(to a crowd of rebels) "He's not a Gunslinger! Not anymore."

Another expressed, "The Gunslingers have sworn an oath, to defend the Tower..."

Roland yells, *"Look around you!* The war is over, and we lost...The Darkness is everywhere. Trying to fight against it accomplishes nothing...There was always a battle, *always!* But no more."

A girl asked, "Is that why we've lost? Because everyone stopped believing?"

"As long as Darkness is out there, the Tower will fall."

"...I kill with my heart."   ~ 'The Dark Tower' (2017)

"Do you recall what I told you of the Convergence?"

"Yes. The alignment of the worlds. It approaches, doesn't it?" Thor asked.

"The universe hasn't seen this since before my watch began. Few can sense; even fewer can see it. The _ effects can be dangerous. It is truly beautiful."

"I see nothing."

"Every 5000 years, the worlds align perfectly. We call this the Convergence. During this time, the borders between worlds become blurred. Once the worlds pass out of alignment, then the connection is lost."

(bad guy) "Your universe was never meant to be! Your world...will be extinguished!"

In the movie, the Dark did not consume the Light.

                    ~ 'Thor: The Dark World' (2013)

The psychiatrist, Dr. Pine, has an older patient, Mr. Darnell, in session...

"...I don't think it's something many people will accept."

"Well. It's my job to understand," Dr. Pine replied.

"...I was curious why things happen the way they do? Those questions no one can answer...I was given the secret [time-viewing/time travel]...and it was so simple..."

"Hm?"

Mr. Darnell said, "Some of the worst crimes against humanity are done with the best intentions. *This was the greatest find in history.* It was bound to revolutionize the way people live, the way they thought. I got the government to listen. They brought me deep inside [bunker], surrounded me with the world's greatest scientists. Not the ones you hear about..."

"Really?"

"...They studied my work, cross-examined my calculations. It was real...the government was at my door, offering me the biggest check I'd ever seen..."

"You took the money?"

"Everyone was looking for the next great leap in technology and this was it! I envisioned a 'window' in time..."

"Like a big screen where you could see history?" ('Guardian of Forever' in Star Trek).

"Yes...Once it was released, publicly, people could see any time they desired without directly affecting past events. It was the only way to keep it safe, so we thought."

"So anybody could see anything?"

"Think of it as *memory recall.* Everyone has experiences they can revisit, even vividly. Now imagine events in time as memories for the world in the space-time continuum. I discovered a way to harness that...(What if they found out?) Jesus was just a man...Imagine the devastation from a revelation like that..."

"Umm." Dr. Pine was stunned.

"...Once the repercussions were being felt, no one could have imagined just how bad it was gonna get...We tried to stop the mass-consumerization of it, plead with the government. But by this time, the damage was too severe, the technology was in too many hands...Of course, you need a *machine* to sustain a wormhole..."

"Please continue."

"Can the ripples I create be enough to change the future or create an alternative one? All of society's mysteries and questions could be answered (viewed). Men looked back and found secrets their governments were hiding; why are the Kennedys being killed? Savage European settlers who stole the country from Native Americans. The truth divided us. The world lost its faith in not only God, but in *everything.* Anarchy replaced order. Destruction."

"You really can't expect me to believe you're from the future? What about causality? Paradox?"

"When you went back, you'd create an off-shoot, like a separate timeline. A new branch of time, moving forward, parallel to the original..."

"Okay. What if somebody went back and killed Hitler?"

"What if Hitler *was* killed?" Mr. Darnell told the doctor pointblank.

"What?"

"What if originally he was killed? And somebody went back and kept him alive? To us, we'd remember it as our history, as if it always happened..."

(Dr. Pine, to a friend) "He said some pretty scary stuff. Look. Let's pretend this guy's the real deal? He comes in and tells me that the **world's gonna go dark in a few years** and everything is severely screwed up. He came back to see what he could do to change it..."

The entire time Mr. Darnell had his sessions with the psychiatrist, a Hindu SHIVA statue was prominently viewed in the background. A much larger version of the Shiva stands near the CERN Collider, which many believe is causing the Mandela. The Moon photo on the wall moved: It was behind him in some shots and also shifted to the wall on his left.

Spoiler: *We discover that Darnell and Pine are the same person.*   ~ 'The Penitent Man' (2010)

[Major Robert Gaines returned from space]. "...And yet it all seems to be some sort of a crazy pattern. Something is very wrong!...When I left here, I was a major...what if, other things..."

(To daughter) "Honey. You know I don't take sugar (in coffee). What's the matter?"

"Nothing."

"Tell daddy what's the matter?"

"Daddy. Daddy, you're different."

"How, honey? How am I different?"

"I don't know. But you are. You're very different! There's something wrong." [runs away].

"Am I, Helen? Have I changed from now to when I left?"

"I can't explain it. You're not the same..."

"I don't know what it is that happened. But something did. Something is tearing us apart. Something so remote, we can't even put it into words."

(doctor) "Really a strange collection of delusions...his own rank...and the last thing he said is he doubted very much if President Kennedy would pin any medals on him."

"President who?"

"Kennedy. Someone named John Kennedy...and I share your bewilderment: I never heard of him either."

(To doctor/friend) "I've been going over a set of encyclopedias and I wrote down some notes. I've uncovered very revealing items. There are some basic historical facts that simply don't jive. For example, talks about a man named Anderson, who was sent by the U.S. Government to supervise the construction of the Panama Canal..."

"So?"

"So I never heard of anyone named Anderson. It happened to be a man named Goethals. It also talks about an American ace named Eddie Rickenbacker from World War 1, who was lost on a raft in the next war and never found..."

"That's right. He crashed and that was the end of it."

"But that *wasn't* the end of it. The raft was found, Rickenbacker *was saved.* He became president of an airlines company. I've got dozens of items like that. Men, talked about who never existed. Men who existed, and not even mentioned? Historical events I know happened a certain way. Somehow, according to the encyclopedia, *didn't happen.* Or happened another way...The things I remember are not delusions. They're the legitimate things, as I remember them. But somehow, some way, this world seems to have turned upside-down for me. Not in every way, you understand. Ah, by in large, the people are the same, the names, the streets...the mutual recollection of people and events. It's as if there were...another world PARALLEL to mine. As if this world was almost a twin, except for some minor differences that happened along the line of evolution..."

Doctor asked, "If all this is true, if you've uncovered that there are two Earths, two sets of people, two histories and you, inexplicably, crossed over to the other dimension? Then you're not who we think you are...and we're not who you think we are."

~Suddenly switched to his twin, back in space...
Major Robert Gaines asked Ground Control: "Who's the President of the United States?"
"Sounds like you're asking who the President is?"
"That's precisely the question..."
[Communication ended]. "I hope you said Kennedy. I hope you said Kennedy..."
He lost consciousness and blacked out...

In a military hospital bed, Major Gaines' head cleared:
The General finally answered his question: "President Kennedy. You were only gone two days, not two years, Major."
"Something happened. I know you're not going to believe this. I'm not absolutely certain that I believe it, myself...There's another dimension. I don't know how it exists or where it exists, but there's another world...parallel to ours. Same people, same places, most of the same chronology of events, except now and then, there's something a little different."
"How do you know this?"
"Because I was there. I was there for a week, General."
"That's *impossible*. We only lost you for six hours..."
"I can't help that, sir. During those six hours, I lived out a week..."
"Doing what?"
"Looking at our counterparts, looking at us..."
"Us?"
"Us. As we exist in a parallel world, one that exists alongside, which we can't see. The world I stumbled into...There's a doorway up there, somewhere, it exists...I think it's possible for somebody to fall through [rabbit hole] it. And I did."
(doctor/friend) "Bob, I think it just may be a delusion?"
"A delusion? I can recount to you every minute and everything that happened...I can recall to you the streets, the places, *everything!* It was no delusion, no dream."

"One last question...if we each have a counterpart, and you saw them? Where was yours, Bob?"

"...I don't know. But he was a Colonel, full-Colonel...I hope he got back."

(Officer to General, in hall) "We got a message from Capcom, sir. It doesn't make much sense..."

"Let me be the judge of that. What was the message?"

"Capcom reports telemetry with an unidentified space vehicle..."

"What?"

"Yes, sir. They had voice communication for about a minute and a half. It was Astro 7. The person in it identified himself as a Colonel Robert Gaines..."

"Colonel Robert Gaines?"

"Yeah, we got some garbled stuff and then there was nothing, the thing just disappeared."

Rod Serling: *"...You can accept or reject...credulous or incredulous. Don't bother to ask anyone for proof that it could happen...prove that it couldn't happen. This happens to be the Twilight Zone."*   ~TZ 'The Parallel' (1963)

(positively-charged Lazarus) "He's mad, Captain. He couldn't live knowing that I existed..."

Captain Kirk said, "So, you're the terrible thing? The murdering monster? *The creature?!"*

The man, with a calm expression on his face, said: "Yes, Captain. *Or he is?* Depends on your point of view now, doesn't it?"   ~ Star Trek, 'The Alternative Factor' (1967)

(Chancellor Palpatine) "Once more the Sith will rule the galaxy...and we shall have *peace*...The time has come. **EXECUTE ORDER 66**."

"It will be done, my Lord."

(Emperor Palpatine) "...In order to ensure the security and continued stability, the Republic will be reorganized into the first Galactic Empire! For a safe and secure society." (applause).

(Padme) "So this is how liberty dies...with thunderous applause."   ~ Star Wars, 'Revenge of the Sith' (2005)

"The future...the polar ice caps have melted, covering the Earth with water. Those that have survived, have adapted to a New World."   ~ 'Waterworld' (1995)

Dr. Ventress: "...The last phase vanished into havoc...I needed to know what's inside the Lighthouse...It's not like us. It's *unlike* us. I don't know what it wants or if it wants. But it will grow until it encompasses everything. Our bodies and our minds will be fragmented until not one part remains. Annihilation!"
                                    ~ 'Annihilation' (2017)

Honorable mentions go to 'Journey to the Far Side of the Sun,' with Roy Thinnes (1969). A literal mirror-twin of Earth in our orbit on the other side of the Sun. Also:

'The Final Cut' (2004) with Robin Williams. "Set in a world with memory recording implants, Alan Hakman is a cutter, someone with the power of final edit over people's recorded histories (memories)."

Blade Runner author, Philip K. Dick: "We're living in a computer-programmed reality. Only clue we have to it is that some variables are changes. Some alterations occur."

Do you know what a "yoda" is to a high-level Freemason? A small demon. There was a reason the creepy character spoke in reverse.

If there is any doubt that a dark, dread, demonic universe is upon us, there are three words that will prove my point: "Star Trek Discovery." Case closed.

One final thought on Predictive Programming in stories. Could be nothing? Remember the Bizarro World presented in early Superman DC comics? Right was wrong. Wrong was right. You said "goodbye" when you greeted someone and you said "hello" when you left them. "Hello."

TS Caladan

***** Bonus short story: *Lightmare*

[The following short story does not take place in our universe or in our mirror-universe. It takes place in another (parallel) world entirely, and its mirror-world].

Eldan Meyer had a strange life up until his fortieth year. At that point, his life went into *hyper,* far into depths of mega-strangeness like he never imagined. He was the Oscar Meyer kid! He sang the jingle on the famous TV commercial in 1967 when he was 10. "My bologna has a first name, it's O, s, c, a, r..." He was heir to the great Oscar Meyer wiener fortune. In fact, Eldan was made President and Chairman of the Board at 38 years of age with the last passing of the New York (hot dog) Meyers.

But in 1997, the man was forced to abdicate his high position, give up his valuable shares of company stock and was basically *fired.* He was fired at gunpoint! You see, Eldan had a heart and was a good man. That cute, curly-haired and very rich, little boy grew up to be a decent human being. He didn't partake in the usual pitfalls of the filthy rich. The unmarried, loner of a man lived as a recluse. Although. When President and Chairman Eldan Meyer discovered what really went into the company's meat products, he was about to 'blow the whistle,' go public and expose everything (before lawsuits rained in, he believed).

That's when GUNS entered the picture! His life would be sacrificed so the company could continue. Or, he could live. He chose to live. He kept his mouth shut. He was unhappy with his decision. Meyer knew what the company was doing was wrong. He vowed someday: He'd make things right, do something great for the whole world, if he could. *Something.* Anything big and wonderful, to change things and make up for his family's sins.

He accepted the deal the Men in Black feds offered him. Eldan went into a CIA program in the LA area. His life reset; he started anew. The man was given a cushy, mid-level job at ZenoDyne Industries, where they were: "Dedicated in finding Future Power Sources."

He was alone, rich, and wandered through life, aimlessly. He searched for meaning in everything. His daily routine consisted of lab work in a fed lab that he thought was prestigious and was actually doing good research, specifically [his department] on the verge of creating what was known in sci-fi as a "Stargate." The possibility excited him, got him out of bed in the morning. He could have spent the rest of his life in comfort, but ZenoDyne intrigued him: Maybe they need not build rocket ships at incredible costs that come with great risk to explorers? Maybe they needed only to step through an artificially-created, mini-wormhole and arrive in a new universe? That was the promise of his department. The possibilities were limitless, if successful. They tantalized him; *his mind was on fire.*

Eldan worked hard on the problem and "burned the midnight oil" during late hours in a lonely quest to save the world. It was on his 40th birthday, after studying countless papers and math equations, suddenly...

The answer was as simple as pie. Or was it as easy as cake? He had it; he knew he had the answer that would create a stable portal or conduit to a parallel world. He tested his idea with the massive, metallic circle that the company often electrically charged to maximum intensity, but always powered down and notes were made. Never was there ever an attempt to electro-magnetically push further, go over the edge and really form the event horizon. Was everything at ZD bogus and only for 'show'?

It was as basic as pulling the prime EM lever all the way into the red. A gateway vortex should form for a few seconds, enough time for him to step through and **GO!**

Why not? He tried it and SUCCESS! His test hamster made the trip without the mammal imploding or dying. Remote sensors sent back data from the Other Side that "Spammy," the hamster, was alive and kicking. That clinched it for Mr. Meyer. He wasn't sure if the journey into the unknown was the redemption he looked for. Didn't matter. It had to be the reason fate placed him here on the edge of the abyss. Tomorrow. He was going to make the leap.

When Eldan got home in the early morning hours, he knew he wasn't about to sleep. This could be his last night on Earth. Well, the last night on the Earth he knew. If all went "A-OK," tomorrow, he'd be alone in the lab in the early morning hours. The tests occurred so often that one more unscheduled surge (like the hamster test) should not be noticed. It also might mean that tomorrow will be his last night *alive?* Who knows how long Spammy's life will be on the Other Side, or his?

Eldan fixed a stiff drink, put on sweet music and simply rested for a good, long time on his soft couch. He smiled, looked around and saw his 5x5 Rubix's Cube that he only realized now he'd never solve. He missed his cat, Sheno. She had passed last month and was another reason that the man really didn't care to move on in this life anymore. He wanted something else now; he wanted FREEDOM or DEATH. It didn't matter which one. No one was more up for *change* than Eldan Meyer.

He laughed. Then he sang the end of a familiar song, "...My bologna has a last name, it's M, e, y, e, r. Ha." He laughed again and raised his glass. "Thanks, old man. Ah." He finished his drink. His mind turned to what he was going to do tomorrow, if he hadn't decided to jump:

He was going to buy one of those new computers. He asked himself: "What was it called, Dial-Up? That might havta wait, until I...*if* I get back, eh?" Then another thought popped into the man's mind. He said, "Oh, that's right. I shouldn't put off the ceremony for another day..."

Eldan got up and walked into the kitchen. He opened the door to the fridge and pulled out a very old, rotten pack of Meyer hotdogs. He tossed them in the microwave and set it on high. The stench was in some weird way *beautiful* to the man. Maybe he was burning his bridges to his past and the world he knew?

Later, he remained pumped with energy. He said to himself, "If I were to watch one last movie out of my vast number of movies on videotape, what would it be? Hmm." Meyer walked over to his shelf of classic films. "Not Casablanca or Citizen Kane. Ah, ha. I know." He liked his decision and laughed. Eldan pushed the 'Wizard of Oz' tape into the player and shouted, "Weeee're

OFF to see the Wizard!" He smiled. It was fitting. What new world awaits?

Tomorrow night turned into early morning. The last person in ZenoDyne's 'Stargate' department said goodbye to Eldan. He was alone. He marched from one desk to another, checked his notes again. He made sure the metal mechanism would hit maximum energy yield for seven seconds, then automatically, and slowly, power down and shut itself off, like before. When all the red lights in a row lit, the Circle would be powered to maximum. That would be the moment to jump.

He was going to do it. Eldan took a big breath and smiled. This was it. All the preliminary procedures were executed.

The Stargate hummed, warmed up and got a bit brighter. Electro-magnetic forces got louder the more Meyer pushed the prime lever. It went into the red. He was excited and pushed harder. And the same result happened: inside the Circle, the vortex formed and a fantastic LIGHTSHOW appeared to the man's eyes. Pulsating, fast-moving bands of energy in blues, greens and yellows, crossed each other in brilliant waves. The machine roared with power!

The critical moment came; the row of lights all lit red!

Eldan Meyer, for better or worse, closed his eyes and leaped through the Looking Glass of Light and Electricity, and into the great unknown...

He didn't land in Emerald City or in Wonderland. His jump out of the Stargate... landed him on the metal ramp of the Stargate? ("Huh?") The amazing lightshow of a spiraling vortex stopped, behind him. There was the sudden power-down of the device that lowered in volume and lowered again. Vibrations decreased...

Silence.

Elden grabbed his gray jumpsuit and made sure all of his body parts were there, intact, and in the places they were supposed to be. He turned back and saw through the circle, exactly like it normally was when not in operation. He walked up the ramp a few steps and touched the metal. It was cooler than he thought. "Wow." He looked around.

The large, mostly metallic room was the Stargate facility at ZenoDyne. No one was around. Everything seemed normal, like he never left. It was 2:30 in the AM. All was as 'quiet as a mouse.' Then, Elden saw it. "Oh, my God! Ha!"

It was Spammy! He ran from one giant electrode to another.

Elden soon corralled him in a corner and picked him up. "Hey, there. Little, buddy. You made it. Ha, ha. Oh, let me..." Mayer removed a sensor attached to the hamster. "There. Ha. That'll feel better, eh?" The man then placed the animal in the palm of his hand and inspected it. He started to pet Spammy, as he'd done a dozen times before. And...

The hamster bit him, hard.

"Augh! Fuck!" The unexpected pain jerked the hamster out of Elden's hand.

Spammy was soft and absorbed the fall without injury.

Mayer bled, profusely. He got a cloth and wrapped his hand. "Never done that before." Eden chalked it up to the little guy must have been frightened or really went through radiant energy where he was damaged. Maybe mentally or psychologically?

Elden seemed fine. In fact, he felt *great,* great and tired. He thought: *Might as well go home.* He captured the little bastard, put him in the Habit-Trail and took him home.

All in all, Elden Mayer was disappointed. He was *greatly disappointed,* the more he thought about it. He wanted *change.* He wanted to reach Nirvana! Some new, alien realm, a different dimension, a Twilight Zone, some brave, new world? He wanted to be an explorer, a hero. But what kind of trick had the universe played on him? He believed he only achieved the same old routine and was back where he started. "Shit."

Later, when he got home to his apartment, and after he found a spot for the Habit-Trail, he undressed and prepared for a good, long sleep. Elden removed his company ID tag from around his neck and tossed it. It missed the dresser and fell to the floor. When he picked it up, Mayer got a better look at the name. "Can't believe it! You mean they can't even get my name right? All this time...and I never noticed? My name isn't *Elden Mayer!* HA!"

[What he didn't know: On the Other Side of the Mirror, it was].

Elden was on his waterbed that he'd slept in for the last 20 years. Something was different, an oddity that (at first) he couldn't explain. Why did the bed appear so large? Why was there less room in the room? He remembered he had a queen-sized waterbed. Why did it appear king-sized? Was it his imagination and the bed always was huge in size? Mayer wasn't sure.

It was 4AM. When he was well-rested and prone upon the fluid softness under him, he focused his thoughts. The room was dark and quiet. Elden contemplated many things in order to understand. He remembered a photo on the fridge that was never there before. It was of him on a boat, smiling, with his arm around a young boy. He wondered: Where was he? What boat? Who's the curly-haired kid and who took the picture?

He contemplated the incredible idea that **his old world was gone** and this *parallel* was a completely different universe. He put the pieces together: Spammy's now violent and he never was before. 'Habit-Trail' was different, Elden remembered the logo was one word, not capitalized. The strange photo in the kitchen he couldn't remember. The waterbed that had *magically enlarged*. The name-tag. "My God." He realized that he *was* within a Twilight Zone, a different reality than the one he left. Maybe he *was* Elden Mayer here? He was fooled into thinking he hadn't left or the power-surge did nothing. He wasn't under a cruel joke. He wanted to leave and *he left*. 'Boy Howdy' did he leave! Here was the ADVENTURE he sought, possibly the chance to put things right? So he hoped...

It was 7AM. Elden caught a couple hours of needed sleep. The Sun had risen. Suddenly, he awoke to noises in his bedroom. *What the hell? He wasn't alone.* His eyes cleared and he watched and listened in horror, or was it total fascination?

"We're home. Toldja I'd be early morning by the time we'd get in from Grandma's." An attractive, brown-haired woman flit from here to there. She bloody well made herself at home. She unpacked a small suitcase and put things certain places. "Hey. Go back to sleep, El. I got a few errands, but you don't have to get up..."

Elden was ready to scream or say something to this stranger, then decided to play it cool. He listened and learned, under the covers of the very big bed.

"Luke *loved* the convention! Ha, he saw tons of creepy aliens. He was so excited, just what he adores. Shudda been there."

Mayer grunted. *(Luke?)*

"He's asleep in his room. All tuckered out, still. Ma was happy to see us. Perfect excuse to visit, her livin' near the convention center. Oh." She bent down and kissed a nearly comatose Elden.

He froze as she kissed him flush on the side of his mouth. The dazed man tried to pucker. He hadn't been kissed in more than ten years, by choice. He thought: *Wow. This is my wife, we're married and we have a child? Wild. It really wasn't the journey I had in mind.*

She rearranged more stuff and undressed at the same time. Off went the bra.

It had been ages since Elden, more like Eldan, saw bare titties. Then the moment was gone....

She changed into black clothes and continued with: "I didn't know Captain Kirk never said, 'Beam me up, Scotty?' *Huh.* It was always a variation like 'Beam us up, Scotty' or 'Beam me up, Mr. Scott.' Never knew that. It was all the buttons and T-shirts that said it, eh? Reminds me of in 'Casablanca,' people still think Bogie said, 'Play it again, Sam.' Nope. Never said it, it was always: 'Play it, Sam, play it, Sam.'"

He agreed, "Ah, huh."

"Also reminds me...remember in college you told me, that during Vietnam, there was a rumor went around actor Jerry Mathers was killed in the war? *The Beaver!* Well, that was wrong; he lived to be an old guy. *Just sayin'*...people believe rumors, things that aren't real, but they make it real because they believe them to be. Hm? El?" She looked at him. Her new outfit in the mirror looked great.

Mayer only uttered one word: "Crazy."

"I know! Watch watcha believe, I guess. I'm babblin', hon." She looked around. "I think I have anything. Oh. I loved the convention, too. Sulu was there, and, and, wait until you see what Vulcan crystals are, my friend. Far-out, ha. Ah. Nothing on the agenda for Luke. It's raining. You two can watch movies or whatever you do when I'm not around? *Okay.* Dude. We'll fuck later. Bye." The pretty girl dashed out of a bedroom bathed in morning light.

(I thought it was raining?) The man waved bye. He only had

his head above the covers. In total confusion, he whispered, "Okay, honey, darling, whatever. We'll *fuck* later." He was spooked. He took a big breath and then exhaled: "Wow."

An hour later, Elden got a good look at his young "son" in the kitchen at breakfast. Luke had much lighter hair than he did. The boy was almost a blonde. It felt wonderful to cook eggs for a son he never had before. The man played along in this dream world. A box of 'Fruit Loops' was on the table.

Later, the boys found themselves around the TV and VCR in the living room. The rain was back and it was the perfect time for movies.

"Hey, matching Sketchers!" Dad saw that they wore the same tennis shoes. He didn't notice that the name wasn't the same.

"'Course. Yeah. You were there when ya bought'm for us? You don't 'member, dad?" The boy seemed bored.

"Oh, right, right, Luke. So....ah, what do you want to watch?" Elden rose to his feet and looked at the movies on one of the shelves. He thought he'd choose for the young man. "Ah. How about? Aaah...Berenstein Bears?"

"Dad! *You know I don't watch that anymore.* I mean, I know was gonna happen..."

"Wait a minute!" The man got a better look at the tape box cover that he thought he knew very well. "No way!"

"What, dad?"

"This has to be a misprint. Maybe a bootleg knock-off? That must be it."

"Huh?" Luke moved closer to his father.

"What? *They're not Jewish, anymore?*"

"Huh? What?"

Elden shoved the cover directly in front of the boy's eyes and asked: "Take a close look at the bears' name, Luke. Was the name always BerenSTAIN, like you make a stain on your clothes?"

"Whaddo you mean?"

Mayer realized: *it could be important.* "Did the bears always have this name, son? This name exactly, the way it's spelled here? Or was it different? Do you recall?"

"I member it like dis, daddy. My Berenstain Bears...you can burn that, you know?"

"Funny. Yeah, I also had a joke about Smokey, you know? *Only you can put out forest fires.* What's Smokey's middle name?"

"Huh? Smokey Bear's middle name?" Luke asked in confusion.

"Yeah. What's the bear's middle name?"

"I dunno. Tiberus. He doesn't *have* a middle name. Dad!"

Elden stated, "It's 'the.' Smokey the Bear. It's supposed to be funny?"

The boy expressed, "I don't get it."

Mayer saw crayons and Luke's coloring book. "Oh, ah. Yes. Luke? Bet you can't spell mommy's name?"

"Sure, I can. What I get? You think I'm a dumb bastard?"

"Luke! *Language!* What do you get? You're gonna get a good spanking if you don't write down mommy's name, perfectly. Here. It's a test." Elden gave the boy a red crayon and tossed the book into Luke's lap.

"Right. Spanking? *You?* All right, I'll do it," he said, reluctantly.

The 4 letters were: 'R,' 'U,' 'T,' and 'H.'

"Ah, like Baby Ruth."

"What?"

"Movie! We can't play outside. You didn't answer what you wanna see?"

Luke's reply stunned the phony father: "You really are a dumb shit if you don't know?"

Elden stood over the boy with his hands on his hips. "What did you say to me, young man?"

"How stupid are you? Don't get all, uh, *fatherly* on me, now. What if Ruthie fown out what ya been doin' to me on our, uh, *camping trips?* Out ina woods?"

Mayer was shocked. It was like the cute kid was suddenly 'Damien.' Did he just turn evil or was he always evil? The boy had to be lying. "I never touched you improperly, Luke."

"Oh, yeah? Yeah? Then who's dick was I jackin'? Who's cock was I...'"?

"MOVIE!" Elden screamed the word so loud at the boy that the kid was scared. The man realized this was a mistake, or was it? Maybe the other Elden *had* molested the boy? The other Elden, or the Elden to his Eldan. The punk little kid may have been victimized by a 'Mr. Hyde' version of himself? It could very well be that Luke was not lying. This could be the Dark Universe, one of anti-matter, where right was wrong and wrong was right? Mayer maintained a firm hand over the ten-year old, terror-child. He demanded: *"What movie do you want to see, Luke?"*

"What I ALWAYS wanna see: Empire Strikes Back....*dummy.*"

Mayer understood, to a degree, that he may have jumped into hell. The "dummy" comment hit him like a rock. Funny, he didn't notice horrible vibes from the wife, Ruthie. Elden got the feeling that the rugrat-monster they spawned in this twisted and upside-down world, was *always a holy terror.* He didn't cause it by the Jump. No. This was a negative universe, a bad one that he now felt. The man wondered: *Would he ever get back home?* Now, he wanted to return. If this weird dream was a nightmare, he wanted to wake up.

Luke took charge. He put 'Empire' in the machine and forwarded the tape to his favorite part in the entire film. "There."

Both sat down. The negative Luke was transfixed to the TV screen as soon as the light came on. They relaxed and watched...

(Luke to Darth) "Obi-wan said you killed my father!" Skywalker yelled as he hung from the tower.

Darth stood over the boy, reached out with his hand and said: "No, Luke. I am your father."

Luke, in the room, was instantly and utterly amazed. "What the fuck? He said my name! He said my name!"

Mayer reacted: "What?"

The boy leaped to the VCR and played the part again. In shock, he heard the same thing. One more time, Luke rewound the tape and played it. "Luke" was heard each and every time Luke played the tape. "That's not right."

Elden was also astounded, not by the tape, but by the violent reaction in the boy.

The 'son' turned to his 'father' with fear in his eyes. He shook. The confused boy tried to understand, but couldn't. "Why'd he say 'Luke,' daddy?"

"Luke. I don't know what you mean. What's wrong?"

"What's wrong? Everything! Last night we saw Mark Hamill repeat Darth's words on Late Show! It was always 'No. I am your

father.' Now 'e's sayin' my name! Dad. It never did dat before!"

"Easy. Well. Maybe you're mistaken?"

The kid just stared at the man and tilted his small head.

After a slight pause, it dawned on the man that this world on the Other Side of the Mirror...*could be changing. Was changing~*

Elden's mind was suddenly blown to pieces when he just realized: *He went home to his apartment. But now, he and his family live in a house?*

"Augh! I'll prove it..." The boy ran off toward his bedroom, then ran back into the living room.

He set a plastic model of Darth Vader down on the coffee table with some force. He held it steady. Luke, with tears in his eyes, turned to his 'dad' and proved the point. "Listen. Wazzit gonna say?"

"Huh?"

The boy pushed the button, like he'd pushed it a thousand times before.

Plastic Vader with his arm out said: *"No. I am your father."*

When Luke pressed it again, it repeated the same words. Then he asked Elden, "What'd ya member, dad?"

Mayer thought: *The little terror-child sang a 'different tune' at the moment; he was scared.* Elden replied, "It doesn't matter what I remember, Luke, what matters is...I believe you."

They shared a moment. The boy hugged him. It felt good.

"Thanks, dad."

Later, Elden Mayer felt the need to walk, get some air, now that the rains stopped. He wondered about his sudden wife. *What'll happen when Ruth gets home, to the house?* Both he and the boy were up for a walk. They got along, no verbal abuse like before and no mention of any other kind of abuse. They walked along the streets of Burbank, California. Beautiful, downtown Burbank of a negatively-charged universe, apparently.

During the walk, the smart and sensitive kid remembered a few oddities: "Shudda known 'cos Froot Loops was spelled wrong; 'Fruit' was spelled right. Where'd the O's go?" Luke noticed: "Our tennis shoes, they're different. And. There was one more, dad. Looney Tunes! Dat's it! I thought: *Why change 'Tunes' to 'Toons,' like cartoons? It was always like music tunes.* But dey now say

'TOONS.' Daa, da, da, da, da, da, daaaaa! Shazam. Ha."

Elden certainly believed the boy and had renewed respect for his point of view. Interesting. The kid's bad attitude sure had changed. Mayer responded with, "Ha. Luke. Well, now you know where the O's went."

Luke laughed. "That's funny, ha." The boy saw another bit of weirdness that caught his attention. He was excited and yelled, "Look dere, dad!" He pointed...

"What?"

There was a big 'JC Penny' store across the street. The boy couldn't help but express: "Fuck, me."

"Language!"

"I'm sorry, dad."

"Now what's wrong? I don't see anything."

"Ya don't? It was 'JC Penney.' Two 'e's. Why change da name?"

"You're sure of that, are you, son?"

"We have catalogs at home. Member?"

"Oh, yeah. You're right. I believe you, son."

At that point, the man glanced through the glass of a cafe in Burbank, while the boy looked across the street. The man couldn't believe his eyes. This was not a weird reality change. He figured it had been going on for quite some time. *He saw Ruth in the arms of another man!* It was her, definitely; she snogged away in a booth. They probably thought no one saw them. Elden was perfectly located and saw them clearly. He dashed to one side of the window, out of their view, and took the boy.

"Hey! What?"

"Question! It's another test. Does mommy have a sister?"

"No."

"Okay. Here's what you get." He reached in his pocket. "Take this (money), go to that stand over there and get us a few drinks, Okay? You can keep the change."

The boy was happy when he saw the bill was 20 dollars. "Thanks! *Huh...*" Luke examined it closer. "Looks diff'rent. Anyway, thanks!" He rushed off.

Mayer shouted, "No soda! Juice!"

"Sure, sure."

Elden spied through the glass again and hid most of himself.

"Yep." They were still going at it, strong. Then they stopped when a waiter approached. "Huh. Wow."

He walked toward the stand and grabbed his juice from the boy.

They walked in the direction of their house.

The man had a thought. He asked Luke, "If I leave you at home for awhile, you gonna be all right?"

"I'm used to dat, dad. Where ya goin'?"

"I think I'll check-in at work, something I need..."

"It's Sunday, dad."

"I know. Could be important."

"Thanks..."

"Hm?"

"Thanks f'seeing what I see, dad."

They smiled.

Elden walked Luke home. Then he headed toward ZenoDyne in the 'Porche,' which oddly was missing an 's' in its name. He was amazed by his sudden son. The child seemed to have turned to the Light Side right in front of his eyes, the positive one that was his old home. Most adults, when faced by literal changes in reality [or timeline] would either deny and fight, or ignore the phenomenon entirely. Maybe he and Luke were of two worlds and were aware of both universes in collision?

On the drive to the lab, he wondered: *If the negative world, here, was changing to the other one, the positive one he remembered...then, by the same token, was his positive world he left going dark, turning to the Dark Side?* The horror was the thought: *The leap may have started a chain reaction where polarities have switched or are in a process of switching, positive to negative and negative to positive?* He wanted to save worlds, not destroy them. Was the guilt he already carried going to be magnified by a billion? Time will tell...

He walked up to the entrance of ZenoDyne.

The old doorman, Joe Tuttle, was not his usual slow, half-dead, miserable self. The wrinkled man in uniform *smiled.* He was cheerful, laughed, was happy to see Elden, as if *thrilled with Life itself!* That was different. They shook hands. *Wow. He seemed alive.*

TS Caladan

Mayer viewed a few (weekend) ZenoDyne workers from various departments inside the large lobby. *Since when did they wear deep blue jumpsuits?* The clothes were always dull gray. He could tell from a distance: they acted differently. They weren't emotionless 'robotoids' that almost mindlessly went through the motions of their jobs. They were happy. They interacted like warm, decent, human beings. They talked, smiled, said, "Hello, how are you?" and meant it. That was different.

"Elden! Just the man I wanted to see. Impromptu visit, aye? Perfect. Walk with me." It was Wallace Gill, one of the big execs and ZenoDyne and head man of the Stargate Project. *What a prick, A1 asshole and his boss.* He always wore black, like Johnny Cash, or Gary Player, or... This bright, beautiful Sunday, he wore WHITE?

"Sure, Wallace." Mr. Gill allowed the *Oscar Mayer wiener kid,* who was once worth a fortune, to call him: 'Wallace.' If anyone had answers, it would be the head of the Stargate Project.

They took the boss' private "chute" and zipped directly to Gill's lush office and tech room in a flash.

The boss beamed with calm, pleasing, positive energy, a little like the doorman, Tuttle. Everyone in the lobby appeared happy, and Wallace Gill was no different. "Boy do I have a few surprises up my sleeve. Can't wait to show you the good news and blow your mind! You *won't* believe it, El."

"I'll bet. Something tells me...I will."

"Ha, ha. This way."

They entered the large techno-office. It was devoid of people. No techs at any of the stations or monitors.

"Take a seat at the main monitor, there."

Elden never saw the 'heart' and nerve-center of the entire ZD complex without people. He sat down in front of the big screen. "Good news, sir? You said."

"Well, ah, maybe not for everyone?" Gill activated a couple of programs and also sat down next to Mayer. He turned to his employee and stared at him directly. "We know you and your son are aware of changes happening to our world, yes? Elden? I'm sure you've surmised we spy on you?"

"Surveillance. Of course, comes with the territory. But these **changes**, sir. Please! What can you tell me?" Mayer nearly pleaded. He had to know his part in the fluid menagerie where reality had become surrealism.

"This is all because of you, El." Wallace informed him, frankly, *right between the eyes.*

"ME?!"

Gill waved his chubby fingers and declared, "No, not really, *you,* El-DAN...the other one, *Elden.* He's the one who made the huge sacrifice; he had the idea at its inception, *brilliant!* He's the one who jumped first. You mirrored him, you see? Ha, ha. And *we* fucking, horrible, hideous animals in a violent, war-torn world of hate and evil witchcraft are, ha, ha! *Are different now.* Don't you see or know or feel what is going on around our globe at this very moment, Eldan Meyer? It's...*lovely.* Ooh. A warm, compassionate vibration. Like a sweet song."

+E.M. was dazed and frightened. Gill was never *nice* before or charming, but now he was. He asked himself, more than his boss: "I am terribly worried to discover what is going on around MY GLOBE, in the other world, my home...at this very moment? Sir?" [Eldan never fully realized what havoc his negative self could cause on the Earth that he loved. His jump was mirrored by his own 'evil twin,' in a sense. The man, only now, comprehended that as this dark world has brightened, his bright world has darkened. And it was all *his fault,* Mayer or Meyer].

Gill had a broad smile on his fat face, a face Eldan had always hated. The boss answered the man's last question: "I could *show you,* on the screen, here..."

"What?"

"What's going on on *your* planet, *vast changes!* Massive, and negative people on my Earth are becoming positive. We see the Light and we sincerely thank you from the bottom of our black hearts, which are enlarging and enlightening as we speak. Love is a wonderful feeling, El, is it not? Actually. Ha. It's the *other one* we really have to thank, the real guy I worked with for a few years. You, uh, *we just met!* You're only a phantom by-product of 'Project Lightwave.' You *do* look like him, though." Gill smiled again, almost a mindless smile of a 'Born Again.'

"Lightwave?" Eldan repeated, dreamily.

"Yes. Oh. *Won't believe this, kid.* Our (changed) Oscar Meyer hot dogs and meats no longer have rat parts in them, anymore. Ha.

Ain't it great? Your world got the shit later than ours. Believe me, your planet was evil, too. Its rulers/controllers, anyway. But it was the *lesser* of two evils. Now things will turn...*upside-down.* Ah. What a beautiful and wonderful service you guys are doing for our world. We're changing, we won't be all anti-matter like before. *We're goin' GOOD!* Ha. Seriously..."

El was even more frightened. He nervously asked: "A-And, m-my world, Wallace?"

"Oh, man. *Your side is going to HELL!*"

"No. This can't be."

"It be. Relative Hell is changing into relative Heaven...and Earthly Heaven is changing into real Hell." Wallace pushed a button and an old clip from 1967 played on the big screen. "Remember this?"

"...*My bologna has a last name, it's M, A, Y, E, R...*" The clip ended.

El's mouth dropped. "I said 'A.' I fucking said: 'A.' That's not right."

The boss told him: "Let me inform you. You are not seeing our world's commercial, anymore. *It was,* but our universe has altered. People here are discovering the 'Hauptman Effect.' That singing, little boy is amazing millions on our Earth because in the old clip, you're now spelling: M-E-Y-E-R. They all remember: M-A-Y-E-R. What I just played for you is special 'residual' and nowhere in this world, anymore. Disappeared, magically, ha. No. But it *is* in yours. You saw how *your world* now sees you when you were 10. And it's blowing their minds as well, buddy."

"Explain Hauptman Effect. If you would, sir?" Eldan asked with keen interest.

"Gladly," replied a kind and gentle Wallace Gill. "Here, people distinctly remember two different, clashing timelines that concerned the 'Crime of the Century,' which was quite awhile ago. Some were positive the Lindbergh baby was found dead and Bruno Hauptman was convicted of the crime. There's 'residue' evidence to support this. While most others agree with our history that the baby was rescued in a stand-off and Hauptman later escaped custody and was never convicted of the crime..."

"What's truth?"

"You should know, El. There is no right and wrong anymore

when worlds collide. Or are in flux. There is only what was, which is gone, and what is now, the transmogrified reality. It's like a beautiful world has descended upon us, overnight, while a demonic one descends upon your Earth, instantly. Very sorry. People here are suddenly aware of the Effect, searching for them on the new Internet, and discovering more and more Hauptmans. Why? Because our universe is actually morphing into yours and yours into mine. Thank the blessed stars."

E.M. was pissed. He withheld his anger. He firmly asked: "Can you show me the changes in my world?" Then he ordered: "Show me."

"Yes, sir," the boss replied, "Before that, I want to show you a few major changes that have occurred here. If that's Okay, *Eldan?* I should call you by your right name..."

"Please, do it." Meyer was serious and curious.

"Hmm. Where do I start? Oh, the *program!* Let me play for you an un-aired documentary, or the first part of it, anyway..."

"What is it?"

"People here are quickly waking up and realizing the change of polarity and actually seeing physical changes before their very eyes. The Hauptman Effect documentary will be aired on all television channels soon and it will not be deceptive in any way. Once knowledge of this wave/vibration, whatever it is, becomes mainstream, the film will go public. It will explain the Effect honestly, that people should not fear this movement to the Light Side. Not to fear, but *accept* the beautiful, unusual things to come. Look..." The right button was pushed. "There you go. The beginning shows the audience an overview of big transitions that have already happened. Later, the documentary examines each one in detail."

"Wow." Meyer figured: *Where did the boss' dark world disappear to?* **His world**, was the answer. El realized that if he looked at the video in reverse, he could discover the bad changes that were now transforming the Earth he remembered...

"Ha. There's a good one. I'll mute and pause. Do you recognize that, my friend?"

"Yeah. I know art. That's Michelangelo's 'Moses,' sittin' with his staff, probably in the Louvre? What's wrong with that? *Oh, wait, wait, now I get it!* So, what's the sudden change from your point of view? Looks right as rain to me."

"Ha. Well, sir. Everyone who has seen it and other changes, have *freaked.* Some are cool about the alterations and accept them. They say they are *'good signs'* and we should not worry about the transition, the alternate reality we're now in. Eldan!"

"Yes, sir?"

"Where the fuck are Moses' horns?"

"Horns? Ha. Sir? Why the *fuck* would Moses ever have horns?"

"Because in my reality, or history, Michelangelo was one talented and very popular *criminal...*"

"Criminal?"

"Yes. The statue was not an homage to the writer of the Pentateuch, it was a mockery at the religious leader. Fabulous work of art, we once thought. Now the 'hornless Moses' is scaring the willies out people who've seen it. It's going 'wildfire' on the Internet. Ah, next. Check it out..." Wallace fast-forwarded the tape.

Eldan stated, "The Lincoln Memorial. I assume it's still in D.C.? Again. I see nothing wrong with it. Wait. Ah. No. This is pretty much as I remember. How is it wrong to you, Wallace?"

"Where's his fist?"

"Fist! Abe, man of peace, ended the Civil War, but I don't know if that's true here? Why in God's name would he be making a fist, which stands for violence and war?"

"Sure did end the 'Great War, War to End All Wars.' It was supposed to mean a firm balance between war and peace, that war was even *necessary* for peace. Where's the 'war,' man? No more war? This is Earth-shaking, especially to the military complex that rules the world, our world."

"Yeah, no war? That would be terrible," said Eldan, sarcastically. "Next?"

Gill moved the tape ahead to...

Meyer yelled: "Mt. Rushmore! Giant heads of the presidents carved into stone. Wyoming is it? Wait, let me take a good look," Eldan said.

Wallace was a bit upset at the relativity in front of him. "El! You're telling me there's nothing wrong with this picture? Seriously! Take a better look."

The man did. In a few seconds, he expressed, "I thought they were all heads, just heads? Lincoln's holding books and Washington wears a jacket? Outside of that, I see nothing wrong with Rushmore."

"You don't, huh? I'm sorry, El. Of course, you don't." Wallace Gill clicked back into his new, cheery, easy self. "Right. This is the one that's driving some people 'Scanners.' Where'd Ben Franklin go? There's only four heads, Elden."

"You're shitting me?! HA! There were five heads? Franklin wasn't a president."

"Neither was he in this universe. Super talented. Why are the ones who really have talent, the biggest rat-bastards of all time?"

"I dunno," El confessed. "Ego? You're telling me he was a super asshole?"

Gill smiled and said, "The biggest! Wormed his way onto Mt. Rushmore and into the hearts of many, praised as a huge hero to most. For such a *fucker* to rise to the stature of the others, who had shreds of decency...amazing. But now...Ben's gone!"

"That means my Rushmore has grown an *extra head?*" The man was in shock.

"There are endless parallel worlds we've discovered. Our Royalty has learned a high-tech means to intersect or *switch polarity* with our Mirror Universe. Instant changes. Skipping grooves on a record. Machines can do what appears as **magic**. Like what is in the 'Potter Harry' series of books. It's real, as you now know."

"So there are slight differences in the changes, from world to world?"

"Exactly. Indeed. You're from our 'mirror' universe. Your Earth probably has five heads, but other Rushmores might not. Some may have had three heads to begin with and no Teddy? Who knows for sure?"

"I thought *you* did? I mean, my world. You gave me the impression you were going to show me precisely what was happening to my planet, on the screen?"

"Sorry, El. Let me clarify. A surprise guest is coming; she'll tell you about, uh, maybe a few *ultimate changes* to the Other Side?"

"She?"

"Before that. I only have two more items to show you, on

tape. Okay? BIG, sweeping, colossal changes! Really blowin' minds here. You ready?"

"Hit me, boss."

Wallace fast-forwarded to the correct place and paused. "One more time. Take a good, hard look. Everyone knows of Giza on Egypt's delta and the three main, ancient, titanic, stone wonders, perfectly aligned with planetary directions. Yes?"

"Wallace, this will look normal to me. I know the difference between GP and second biggest: Kafka or Chefin pyramid? Chefin is most distinctive from a distance with like a big 'nipple' on top, that are original casing stones. I know that much. Nothing wrong from my view."

"Nothing wrong, huh? People are *losing it* here because of the new arrangement." Stargate boss stopped the image on a front view of the Sphinx with one of the pyramids behind it. "Sphinx has always been aligned with middle pyramid, Kafka, you called it, second largest...*NOT the Great Pyramid!* We have a history where the Sphinx exactly dates to the time of Chefren, the one that was always in the middle. Now look at it!"

"Wallace. Huh. This picture looks weird to you...because Sphinx is now lined up with the Great Pyramid, in center? And, and, no longer close to the city?"

"Yes!"

"Wow. See, to me, I remember it this way. Great Pyramid, the one with amazing/high inner chambers, from older time period when we were *more* advanced, placed right in the middle, center stage. Far from the city. And aligned with the Sphinx. It was Kafka off to the side."

"What can I say, El? You must be from the Light Side. Hey. I don't even want to tell you our Lady in the Moon has been oddly replaced by a *Man in the Moon?* Shocker."

Meyer would have laughed if he wasn't desperately worried about his Earth. Then a strange thought entered his mind: Funny, *he had no one back there. No one he cared about and no one who cared for him. At least, on this side of the Mirror, he had a wife and son.*

"You Okay? Lost in thoughts?"

He asked, "You mentioned a girl, woman. She has answers for me?"

"One more, Eldan. Much bigger than pyramids changing positions overnight."

"Bigger? Continents have changed?"

"YES! I'll let the film play and you can hear the narrator, see the images..."

The Hauptman Effect documentary showed old and modern maps of South America, one after another (and residue of the way it was). A female voice said:

"As incredible as it sounds, to all appearances, the actual land mass of South America has shifted more than a thousand miles west! Almost unanimously, we remember South America far east from where it is now. Today it is located right under North America. People remember the Panama Canal ran a bit north and south. Now it runs east and west. South America is farther from Africa. The Atlantic Ocean seems wider and Pacific a little smaller. Other areas have changed because of the Hauptman Effect. New Zealand was always called the 'land down under,' but has shifted to the north. Now Australia is the 'land down under.' New Zealand was always two islands, now it's one. Sicily is farther away from the 'boot' of Italy. There's an enormous ice cap with land at the North Pole, when before H.E., it was only an ocean. Islands have suddenly disappeared off the coast of California and Australia: Where'd they go? Also, there are many reports of land masses appearing when nothing was there before. As far as American states: There's only a single Michigan now. California, So. Carolina, Wisconsin and Pennsylvania have enlarged, while Ohio and W. Virginia have shrunken in size. West Virginia is now totally south of Pennsylvania and Minnesota has completely lost the small spike of land on its Canadian border. Cities have physically transformed and so have the people...it seems, as if under a spell of positive White Magic..."

The boss stopped the tape and jumped it to the end. A project-logo appeared as a still on the screen. It was the last frame in the documentary. It read: 'Lightmare.'

Eldan pointed at it and asked, "What's that? That's not good."

"It is good. It is informing the audience that a feature film will be produced called 'Lightmare.' You know, another example of 'Predictive Programming'? Only people'll be well informed by the story as a beautiful agenda will be given to the masses, softly.

The film, named after the secret project at Stargate, like the documentary, will help prepare the way for the new world of love, understanding and doing things the right way. Non-violently. No more need for mass-military. No nukes, we will totally/globally disarm. We'll have all the clean, free energy we could ever use, eh? No more kings and queens and dictators. No more fascism or war or World Orders. Real peace. We'll utilize Tesla Technology, *for everyone!* Not just the elite. That certainly will be a first: Power given away to the masses< We'll have a *New Order,* but it will be a simply *marvelous* New Order. A good, one-world government of Global Democracy. We really will have the Dawn of a New Day, a kinder/gentler world. Truth, no more lies. And. We have *you and him* to thank. Did you know you and your family are *celebrities* here? If you want, El?"

"No, thank you."

"What are you going to do? You've thought about jumping back, eh? Yes?"

"Yes. I have, Wallace. That means: he'd bounce over to this side, right?"

"You don't want to do that, my friend. I won't let you. You CAN'T go back..."

The man was fearful. "W-Why not? *What have I done to my world?"*

"El. When I said your counterpart, my dark friend I worked with, the other you, who devised 'Project Lightwave,' made the ultimate '**sacrifice**,' I meant it. There's no...Oh...I should let her tell you. She's here..."

"Who?"

Gill nodded in a direction. "See the White Door? Strange. It used to be black."

"Sure. Shall I?"

"Yeah. Go through it, Eldan. She'll tell you...what she wants to tell you, I guess?"

The man got to his feet and stretched. He turned toward the door. He took his first steps and said, "That's vague, Wallace."

"Have a good life, kid," his boss said seriously and sincerely. He waved goodbye.

They smiled.

Eldan returned the wave and went through the white door...

Inside, was a big round room, all white. In-laid patterns, fantastic designs were laced throughout the floor, curved walls and ceiling. In the very center was a raised circular area more than 30 feet in diameter. In the very center of the round stage, there appeared to be a 3-foot hole. *What was this bizarre, bright room?*

Eldan walked toward center. He eventually stepped up upon the round platform or stage. He slowly eased closer to the exact middle and stood over the black hole, the only darkness in the room. He peeked into it. *What was it? Was something down at the bottom?*

Then he felt a different vibration around him and almost heard a low hum. Suddenly. It seemed like magical sparks or 'fairy dust' snapped and glittered in the air above the hole. A *form* appeared as a misty column. It swirled and turned counter-clockwise and enlarged more and more. Something was coming into the material world and quickly came into reality....

It was a brilliant, old woman. OMG. It was the *fucking Queen of England!* Elizabeth in a gown that (*I think*) belonged to Glinda, the Good Witch. *Shazam!*

"Your...*Majesty?*" He bowed, ever so slightly.

She hovered over the hole and slightly bobbed up and down in the air. Elizabeth said in a meek, British accent: "Now, now, boy, we'll have none of that rubbish. I am no Queen. I am a real woman, from birth, strangely enough. I never was before, dear...El. Are you aware 'El' is Hebrew for 'god'?"

"Ah...no."

"This black ritual room used to summon demons, put evil spells on people or just make them attracted/repulsed to the wrong things. Also located in top music studios and political arenas. That was yesterday, aye? Take my hand, dear," she gently commanded. She smiled again. The former Evil Queen (Wicked Witch, from House of Vlad the Impaler) reached out her tiny, withered hand.

He grasped it and instantly felt warmth, love and real grace. Eldan was in awe. He looked deep into her old eyes. Tears were in his eyes. "Wh-what...should I call you?"

"Please. Please call me 'Liz.' I have a question."

Their hands broke a bond as the man was overwhelmed. "You can ask me anything, your...Liz."

"What horrid, ugly, vicious, wicked stories have you heard

about me, dear boy? I won't call you: *my Pretty.* Please be honest."

Eldan rubbed his chin and took a few seconds to respond. "I looked a few things up when I had a chance to use the Internet. You, other royal families, the Vatican, Mafia, CIA, corporations and other nefarious organizations. That was in *my* world, of course. Specifically, ah, missing children, blood-sacrifice rituals, witchcraft, New World Order, Illuminati stuff...like that."

"I will spare you the gory details. I simply want you to know..."

"Yes? Liz?"

"...That was the *other one.* I never drank blood and pledged allegiance to Satan. I'm the good one. Ha." One more smile.

Eldan changed the subject to what pressed upon his mind. "So...*because of me,* my world's fucked, huh?"

"Ah. Yes and no. This world's Elden Mayer was *played like a fiddle* along with everyone else. It truly is a beautiful place here now on what was once your reverse and negative side of the Mirror-worlds. All double-helixed universes are not the same, you see? Among our pair, one had to be sacrificed. One had to go. One universe had to die and one had to live, beyond year 3000. If no Project Lightwave, *both* would have been destroyed, yes? I'm sure you understand. We built the devices, jumped first and started the Hauptman crossover. We made sure a lovely world survived. Forever."

"And I can't go back to my Earth?"

She sighed and sadly expressed, "You wouldn't want to, Eldan. My evil twin on your world, which is who I was only a short while ago, really *accelerated* the Portal to Hell...that opened other portals to hell. Every time there was a big jump or little jump, like in your films, a darker and darker universe descended upon your world. Time has drastically sped up there to beyond the year 3000..."

"What? You mean, if I had jumped back, it would be in the far future?"

"Far worse, dear boy. Your world has no future beyond year 3000. A lifeless planet that would very soon have killed you."

Meyer stood still and stunned. He stared at the fancy, white floor. "But..."

"Try to look on the bright side, El."

The man raised his head and saw her smiling face. "Huh?"

"We are on the road to utopia here and will achieve it soon. This empire won't fall. Earthly Paradise will have no Other Side or negative side that beckons, teases and eventually swallows it up into corruption. This world, *the world,* is now stable, solid, *real* and will not shift or ever change polarity again. The Earth isn't fake and people care. We will survive in technological and spiritual greatness. What wonders await! You see...only one of the Earths could have continued into the future, beyond the third millennium..."

"Really?"

"...Make the best of our positive realm that no longer has a particle of anti-matter in it or bad vibration, Sir Eldan. New Kingdom is for everyone. Power to the people!" Good Witch smiled a sincere smile, again.

Eldan thought of his wife and son. He just might take Liz's advice.

Both citizens thought it was time to go home. They shook hands again and left: Liz, by way of technical 'magic' (beamed), and Eldan, by way of a Porche hover-car. Now, he owned a hover-car. Nice. This side of the Looking Glass might not be too bad.

He went to his mansion on top of the hill, to his beautiful wife and blessed son.

He decided he would experience all the good things in life that he'd missed, previously. Eldan very much enjoyed the time spent with Luke.

Spammy the hamster, now "Spammy the Details," got along great with the cat, Eno.

Eldan understood that this wonderful Ruth was not the wife that cheated on him (the other him). She had no memory of any indiscretions. Perfect. That evening, the famous couple made love on a king-sized waterbed. They were very happy~

☯

The following two+ short stories combined into one were written to illustrate a point. They are a few more tales based on the Mandela Effect or inspired by the phenomenon...

~ Brothers from Costa Rica and the Buddhist Priest

The time was 2:30 in the afternoon on the last day of the year: 2018. Javier Mendez drove to the California State Prison facility in Lancaster, CA. He arrived a bit early. His brother, Julio, was going to be released at precisely 3PM. He wanted to be there for his brother, pick him up, drive him "home" to father, after a two-year stint in State prison.

Julio wasn't a violent man. He'd fallen in with the wrong crowd, hard drugs were involved. It seemed like from 2016 on, Julio had totally changed personality. Maybe it was the cocaine and crystal meth that changed him? Maybe it was something else?

His father and brother noticed a definite move to the Dark Side in the young man. The kind father was thankful for Javier, "the good son," and did his best to help oldest son. But nothing was going to derail Julio from street gangs, selling and using hard drugs, wild night life and the inevitable prison sentence.

That was the past. It will be the new year of 2019 soon. The Mendez brothers and their father, from Costa Rica, thought tomorrow might be bright. Julio finished his sentence. Javier was to be married in the near future. The father was hopeful.

The long drive to the Mendez house in Van Nuys was uneventful. Little was said. Julio appeared to Javier as the same bald, street punk that he ever was. Prison did nothing for him except made him harder, colder. Javier was sure Julio would have his usual connections and be smoking the glass pipe in no time. *Getting a job* would not be a high priority for Julio. Father would have his hands full with oldest son very soon.

Why? Why was one son responsible, a decent human being, had a good job and an overall nice guy...and the other son was a virtual monster?

When they arrived home, father greeted the wayward son and decided on a big feast the very first evening the brothers were together. No incidents? Maybe? Julio would be on *best behavior.* They enjoyed the delicious food, especially Julio.

Later, the caterer left, and the Mendez family retired to a large living room. They fixed drinks and relaxed. Everyone was pleased. No one spoke of what happened in the past.

Father had no intention of pressuring Julio into a job, not just yet. Although, he knew it would be the best thing for the man. They laughed. They drank more and had a wonderful time.

Julio lifted a glass and made a sincere speech. They all drank a toast to better days ahead.

Javier had heard those words before. He realized his older brother was a conman and will always be a salesman, a schmoozer and a downright liar. Julio would do anything to get what he wanted: booze, women and drugs. It was only a matter of time and big brother would be back in prison.

In father's mind, he knew it too.

That first evening, sweet memories were recalled, passed-on mother/wife was remembered and a few tears shed.

The boys, on the big family couch, remembered a game they'd played in their youth while on vacation: a Geography game. Javier [computer programmer presently] and Julio were not the brightest students in their high school class. But they knew Geography. They didn't know math or history well, but they knew where countries were. They really knew the Caribbean and the Cayman Islands. Father and mother took them on tours around the Gulf of Mexico when they lived back east. The game was to guess how far the ship was from their original home in San Jose. After the boys guessed from different ports, father tracked where they were on the map and saw which son was closest.

All went well that first evening together. Not a word was uttered how different and dark Julio was from the person he was 5 years ago. Then something strange was said by Javier when he recalled the good times the family had experienced...

"We had fantastic vacations in the islands, father. Beautiful seas. First stop on east coast, Port-Au-Prince. Ah. I'll never forget it."

Julio interrupted, "Don't mean to correct you, little brother..."

"Huh?"

"Haiti is on the west coast. Port-Au-Prince. West coast. We've been there a few times."

Javier was not in any mood to argue, not on the first night. He raised his glass and chalked it up to *someone's* mistaken memory. "Whatever, dude."

"Okay."

A thought just occurred to Javier. "Julio. Remember when we

stole the boat? *What we?* It was *your* idea to do it, guy. I just went along with older brother..."

Father laughed, "I remember. Ha, ah. You two serving time in jail. Together. Taught you a lesson, eh? I wasn't going to bail you out, ha."

Julio laughed also. "That was precious. The good son, in jail for three days?"

"Yeah, thanks. That's on my record," Javier said, slightly drunk. "Shit. Yeah, I confess. I wanted to take it out too, but for *only minutes.* I actually thought we wouldn't get caught. And, and, it, it was going to be...fun."

"Fun?" Father chucked.

"You had a good time, Jav. You had a *great* time, I remember," Julio said and raised a glass.

"Bro, I was screaming 'that's enough! We gotta take the boat back!' No, you drove it the whole day..."

"I did not," Julio declared with conviction.

Javier replied, "Huh? Hey, guy. Of course you did. We, I mean, *you,* took the 'New Pinta' and dragged us around the whole fucking island! Dude, that's a many-hour trip in the small rig. Remember?"

"What the hell are you talking about, little brother? You mean the one time we hopped onboard the 'New Pinta," started it up and headed out to sea? For an hour."

Javier was surprised and replied, "There was only one time we were arrested by the Coast Guard, right?"

Julio was baffled. "But you said 'island.' What island?"

Father looked on with curiosity.

"What? *What island?* The island we were born on!"

"We weren't..." Julio grabbed his chin. He contemplated the most unlikely question: *Was he born on an island?* He hesitated, then was sure he was *not* born on an island. "Wait, wait, wait a minute..."

There was a moment of confusion in all three Costa Ricans.

"Julio. Hang on. You said 'hour.' You really think we had the boat out for only an hour that day?"

"Definitely. I wanted to take it out longer. But Coast Guard guys came and stopped us, handcuffs and all that. It was no longer than an hour, Jav..."

"Dude! It takes a lot longer than an hour to circle the island..."

"WHAT Island?!" Julio screamed.

Javier screamed back: "Costa Fucking Rica! That's what island. Dude! You've been locked away too long. What have they done to you for you to not remember?"

Julio turned to his kind father for some relief here. Certainly, he'd clear the air and solve a simple, little problem?

[Where do Costa Ricans come from, an island or not?].

Father laughed. "You're kidding?" He looked straight into Julio's eyes. He asked, "You don't know? Son, you have to know."

The ex-con son stated, "I know I was born in Costa Rica and it's not an island. You, you *seriously don't know* it's on the mainland connected to Nicaragua and Panama?"

Father shook his head.

Javier said, "No, it's not. We..."

The old man got up and walked to a bookcase. "I'll show you on the map, number one son." He grabbed a world atlas from a shelf and turned to the right page of the Caribbean area. Father did not take a close look at the page. He confidently placed it on the coffee table and in front of the boys. "There. Son (to Julio) What do your eyes tell you?"

Javier gasped. He quickly grabbed the book off the table and brought it closer to his face. "Everything's wrong. What?" He looked closer, where CR was now located. He knew those towns. He had a worried expression and shook his head from side to side. "F-Father." He stared at the old man and handed him the atlas.

Father laughed again. He'd spent five decades in Costa Rica and more than a decade in the states. He grew up there. He fished in beautiful, clean, turquoise waters. He'd been off the island and returned dozens of times, vacations with the wife and sons. Father knew he and *his father* spent most all of their lives on the Island of Costa Rica.

Javier was amazed. He grabbed his head. "It's not there, father."

The old man examined the map carefully. He jumped to the cover and date of the book to make sure it was his old atlas. It was. There was no Costa Rica island that once stood southeast of Mexico and southwest of the Cayman Islands. "What? I don't believe it."

Julio laughed a hardy laugh at his absurd father and brother, who should have known. He said, "It's where it's always been: bordering Nicaragua and Panama." The older brother smiled. He said, "See. Right there." He pointed at the map and smiled again.

The year was early 2016. At the "largest temple in the world," the Wat Phra Dhammakaya in Thailand that happens to resemble a gigantic 'flying saucer,' an American student approached one of thousands of praying, Buddhist priests. The bald, orange-robed chap seemed friendly enough to talk to; his face, closed eyes, expressed a sweetness and tenderness as if the man possessed the power of understanding. The student hoped so. He had quite a "magical" question for the wise priest. The student was clueless what the response would be. He quietly stepped closer...

The American waited. He breathed deep breaths. He looked around. He was astounded by the incredible temple, especially with this first near visit, so close to the thousands of golden Buddha statues that surrounded the huge structure. It sure resembled a flying saucer, parked on the edge of a sacred lake. Breathtaking scenery, tall trees and wonderfully designed buildings in the huge complex.

Earlier, it took the student more than 20 minutes to complete one circuit around the disk-shaped temple. He saw the four large openings at the cardinal points. An enormous red flag with a spaceship silhouette adorned each entrance. The student only viewed the Wat Phra from a great distance, mainly his apartment, two miles away, across the lake.

He kept a close eye on the priest of his choice. He'd wait until his meditation, chanting, prayers were over. When the Buddhist opened his eyes, that's when he'd step forward and ask the questions he was desperate to ask.

You see, from the student's perspective, the entire complex of the "Dhammakaya Cetiya" suddenly *appeared one day* in the distance from his window! For weeks, his work kept him home and busy at school. Only today, long after he first noticed, was he able to approach the magnificent "mirage in the desert" that *mystically appeared?* The man had to have answers, logical/sensible answers to how this could have happened.

The student certainly asked around the local area of Hat Yai. Almost everyone he talked to were well acquainted with the "Cetiya," which looked like a giant mothership. It had stood there for five decades. But from the student's viewpoint, it had 'landed' only a short time ago. The oddity was, when he polled enough of the local natives, he discovered a few that were equally amazed as he was. To them, the grand temple had also magically materialized overnight. He'd actually seen fights break out between those who've known of it for decades and other "insane" people that remembered it suddenly, strangely, appeared one day.

He had to talk to a worshiper to sort out the madness. Why did a few of the locals recall, as he did, that the "Cetiya" simply materialized, while others claimed they had worshiped at the temple all their lives?

The priest opened his eyes. He seemed finished with his prayers and was about to leave.

The student carefully, slowly, sat next to the priest.

Smiles were exchanged.

The bald Buddhist was also curious. He remained seated.

The man introduced himself. "Excuse me. Sorry to bother you. My name is Sam. I'm a student from the United States..."

"Yes. I can see that," the priest said in perfect English. He had a pleasing expression on his bright face. "My name is Sura."

Sam pointed to the two-mile distance, where his apartment was located across the water. "Well, Sura. I've lived at the Hat Yai Hotel for a couple months now. I've finished my classes and will be going back to the States soon..."

"How can I help you?" the relaxed, contented man replied.

Sam laughed. He pointed at the massive temple in the other direction and asked: "Ha. Does that fly?"

The priest laughed so hard, tears nearly formed in his brown eyes. "HA, ha! Ha, ha." The robed man decided on a joke. He said, "Ha. Not yet."

Sam laughed again. Then his thoughts became audible: "That, of course, wouldn't explain all the golden statues, now would it? How many Buddhas are there?"

The priest chuckled once more and said, seriously: "Uh.

There is only one Buddha."

"No, Sura. Ha. I mean, the golden statues. God, how many are there around the spaceship, I mean, temple?"

The definite response was, "Three hundred thousand and one."

"Wow. Ah. Question. Are you aware that...to many, *a few people, anyway*...the holy temple has suddenly appeared, like out of nowhere? I'm, ah, asking...have you heard of such things and can you explain it?"

"Explain what, Sam?"

"Er, ah, *why* most remember the temple being here for a long time, while others are bewildered, and think it has just arrived? Sura. To some people, this, all of this, *just appeared."* Sam pointed again. "You know?"

The priest told the student the truth: "You, or they, must certainly be mistaken. Fanciful thought, that the Cetiya and the statues have appeared in an *instant,* as if out of a puff of smoke, eh? Ah. But, I assure you, young man: Construction of the temple took many years to complete, and we have our founders, Chandra and Luang, for the existence of the Cetiya. I have prayed here, along with countless others, for more than ten years. So much peace has been generated from this location, and felt by all who meditate here. No one here is unsure or has divergent views of the temple's solidity, where it came from. We are not confused."

"Sura. Then, uh, how can you account, or answer why many in the area believe the Cetiya has...*just appeared*, like out of a dream?"

The priest smiled a big smile and said, "Huh. Maybe, it did?"

☯

Two mates from Wellington, New Zealand stood on top of a high peak, a place they knew very well from childhood. Of course, Palmerston was to the north, Christchurch to the south and Nelson was to the west. One of them, *just now,* saw a paradox in front of his eyes and was amazed, *while his mate could not see it.* They argued.

"It's right there, man! What's wrong with you?"

"Yer daft! One island? Cook's Strait has always split North

Island from South Island!"

"No! It was never there before. *There's no north and south islands!* A town was there, mate. Called Cook. You remember Cook? We drank in Cook's pub. Now look at it!" He couldn't believe what his eyes beheld: a large waterway had suddenly appeared, from his point of view. And *his old friend didn't view it the same way.* "That's just...*wrong.*"

His mate laughed and repeated a New Zealand expression: "Go back to Canberra."

"Where?"

TS Caladan

****** A few more "oddities." One I've noticed, from my frame of reference, over the last 10 years, that no one else has ever mentioned, to my knowledge. Probably not a Mandela Effect, but I wouldn't doubt it is part of an overall plot to *harden us*. Hear me out.

I refer to the disappearance of wall-to-wall carpeting. I don't know if there's much call for wall-to-wall carpets in carpet stores these days? Sales must be very low. **Wall-to-wall carpeting does not exist in recent movies or television anymore!** Have you noticed? They've been gone for many years, from Seinfeld to Shark Tank. I believe this is a conspiracy, a Media-pushed agenda to make us *hard inside.*

We only view hardwood floors, over and over again, everywhere. Over Media, there really is no exception to the rule. Count. On TV, flick station to station, commercial after commercial. "Oooh. Beautiful hardwood floors. How classy." Throw rugs, Asian rugs, tossed onto hardwood floors and this is the height of sophistication? Wouldn't it make sense for filming? Thick carpets, would be better, quieter? Nope. They are gone.

[Pet peeve of mine. I've never lived in a place that didn't have wall-to-wall carpets. They weren't *great* W2W carpets, but they were wall-to-wall carpets].

What's wrong with you rich people? You'll buy a new car every year, but you can't replace a lush, plush, thick, soft, wall-to-wall carpet? So *that's why* the rain forests have disappeared and where it went! All because you have to be like lemmings (see below) and be the same as everyone else? *So high-class.* They've conditioned you to love being the same cold/hard people without an ounce of compassion. If they had their way, your floors would be made of iron. Doesn't that sound lovely?

Feng Shui.

Our environment affects us. Study dome-creator, Buckminster Fuller, who believed we're not nouns, *we're verbs.* Energy. Tesla also. Physical shapes around us move us as well as invisible frequencies beamed at us are everywhere in the atmosphere.

[Good advice: Rest, relax, sleep and meditate within a Faraday Chamber, which blocks all frequencies. Find out how to build one on YT. We should be living in domes and thinking in curves. But we are forced to live in cubes and think like blockheads].

I first noticed the love of hardwood floors and an end to wall-to-wall carpets in New York many years ago. It seemed everyone lived in a brownstone and, without exception, had hardwood floors. I could be wrong, but I think they're making us tough and violent – when we should be true to our real nature, which is warm and fuzzy. If I was rich (not going to happen), I'd have one room in my dome home as a meditation room, but it wouldn't just have wall-to-wall carpeting, it would have full floor-to-ceiling carpeting as well, thick and plush. *I want to see the guy on the ceiling kick that claw-thing.*

Also. Very important. If you've learned anything, learn this:

Boil your water! Cool it in the fridge. Cook with it, make ice cubes with it and give it to your pets. Do not drink tap water, filtered water OR BOTTLED WATER! Do not! There is still fluoride in bottled water, like in all fruits and vegetables from stores. It's been in our drinking water since the '50s. If you want to clear your head, sharpen your mind, open your Third Eye of understanding, be less susceptible to Media suggestions, free yourself and basically put on the 'They Live' sunglasses, eventually...

Boil your fucking water! Your eyes will focus in time...and mind. You might reach understanding, which is a very peaceful state of being. Happiness.

An oddity that might not be attached to the Mandela phenomenon at all, but is something to think about. It concerns the (British) myth of lemmings, their activities and, more importantly, what we *think* the activities are of lemmings. You know, lemmings? They're a specie of furry "arctic rodents" that fascinate the Brits, for some reason. Ask anyone: "What do [stupid] lemmings do on top of mountains?" And they'll jolly well tell you: "Lemmings jump off cliffs, mate. One after t' other, in a line. They jump to their deaths. One does it, they all has to do it, right?"

An old, colored photograph from some British magazine was placed online. What it showed and stated in the caption shocked me. *I think it revealed the truth.* The camera view was perfectly situated to look down rocky cliffs to the sea. The photo, unbelievably, captured a lemming or two that fell to sure death, far below...and a lemming in mid-flight in the foreground that blindly followed the ones out in front? *["Stupid gits"]*.

Here's the thing: The caption exposed what really went on in the old British photo. They were used for propaganda in papers to perpetrate the myth of follow-the-leader lemmings. There was, supposedly, off-camera, a lemming-catapult or round/wooden thing that, one after another, *shot lemmings off the cliff and down to their deaths~* Wow. Like a lemming-gun or tennis ball-gun. This could be true. Flood Media with this crap that it is perfectly normal and natural to be just "Another Brick in the Wall" and be the exact same as everyone else? Do what everyone else does? *It's in nature and, therefore, in our human nature?*

No, it's not. We're individuals. "If John jumps off a bridge, does that mean you have to, too?" Wait a tick. You mean lemmings *don't* throw themselves off sea cliffs and die in mass-suicides? That's the actual truth. They don't do that. Nature is not that dumb. (But people will believe what they are told, no matter what the truth). They're making us 'Walking Dead' "robotoids," who'll accept any horror handed us, without question. "Experts," most with English accents and origins, will inform you that lemmings have a "migration pattern" that forces them off high cliffs. They have attached the (myth) pattern of lemmings to the psychology of humans. *Experts* have written "prestigious" papers on the subject. Pure bullshit. Pure propaganda, psychological operations *(psy-ops)* and programming. Also known as Human Engineering. Always from England.

Real scientists, if any, would expose the myth of lemmings, not add to the lies, the hoax thrown upon the public. [Same with Darwin]. There are sources today that reveal the truth about lemmings and other things. But they always seem to be in the great minority, don't they? The smallest voice possible.

This book is like 'Ripley's Believe it or Not.' The contents are astounding and you want to check out the truth to extraordinary things. We can today, instantly, with Google and YouTube. What we discover is not how stupid we are or how miss-informed we have been. We find out how much the world we distinctly remember has mutated into something else. Or, I should say, a part of the population does. The difference between my "analysis of a worldwide phenomenon" and Ripley's collections is his weird oddities had always been around. *They were true.* Strange things, little-known facts, very few people had ever heard of. In the case of the present reality, the Mandela anomalies have only showed up or materialized in the last 5 years. Hard to believe, I know. Full histories of jets with thrusters way out in front of wings or Mickey Mouse always without suspenders, Scarecrow's gun, 6 Village People, 6 Jacksons, etc., etc. Ancient sites and super statues, brand new to our eyes, never existed previously, here. Tartarian Empire was never around before. Only in the last 5 years has it existed in reality, our reality...

Believe it or not.

I wanted to insert a statement on: How do we revolve apparent paradoxes and the seemingly fragmentation of reality that sits before our eyes and in our memories? As suggested, we can no longer insist this is true, the only truth, or that is a fact, definitely. Not anymore. I enjoyed one answer to the problem, how Enrique C. chose to resolve the contradiction of Costa Rica island: He understood the stories that his stepmother told him as a child were true...and there was another truth: CR also bordered Panama on the mainland, today. Both universes existed and were real, *somewhere.* It was a beautiful resolution. Maybe we can learn a few things from the young man?

A final comment that you'll never believe. No Mandela, just a plain and simple truth that's a hard pill to swallow: **There were never cowboys**. Never! No macho men at the time would ever be referred to in the feminine. *Cows are feminine, boys!* (It's a Hollywood/British joke on us yanks, like "gay" or "queen"). They would be "bullboys," "bullmen," "horseboys," "horsemen," "rangers," "homesteaders," "pioneers"...

Anything but "COWBOYS." No one, back then, ever called themselves: "cowboys."

Why do we think they did and that there were cowboys? From the first silent cinema that is over 100 years old, totally ruled by the Monarchy's minions, to the first 'talkies' and to the first television shows. Brits were primarily portrayed as sophisticated, cultured, educated and of the upper class. But yanks were the crudest, rudest, roughest, most violent and rootin', tootin' and shootin' characters the West had ever seen. ('Go West, Young Man' and 'Wild West' were code for San Francisco and being gay, like the Hollywood Industry and elites). Movies and television were ruthlessly and secretly installed by Big Brother dictators [Tavistock Institute], to do far more than only watch you:

One-Eye of Britain always has and will continue to mold you millions and billions of its slaves, keep you busy/poor and dying in bogus wars. Soap opera politics are a diversion; they are like Studio Wrestling, *phony*. Its purpose [Media/news] is to keep you entertained, programmed, off balance, arguing and at war. So you don't know the truth of what's really going on and storm the High Castles of the few who dominate you.

Each and every Citizen deserves the advanced technology they've stolen from us. We deserve the Good Earth and the right to be off the "prison planet." You deserve the very best Life has to offer...

You. Not them.

What we believe, we make real.
They control what we believe.
They control what is real.
Discover what is true and *feel*.
Open your eyes. All of them.
Find out for yourself.

"You cannot teach Experience." ~ Siddhartha

Your comments & questions are welcome.
Contact Tray at: **tscaladan@gmail.com**

******* Other books by TS Caladan
http://www.twbpress.com/authortraycaladan

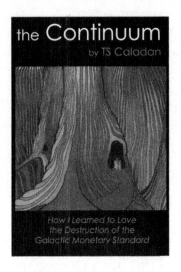

The CONTINUUM My first novel is an epic. I wanted 'The CONTINUUM' to be a broad, sweeping story that is a world of many worlds or "continuums." Zog is God, a super being from very long ago. Parallels to our real world exist in that a great evil (alien) called a "Sardon" assumes galactic power as "Chancellor," similar to Hitler. It is a soulless, ugly, cosmic accountant. Basically, a Devil and negative counter to the perfect Zog-being. Sardon creates the Chancellery and imposes the Dylar upon his galactic empire of many solar systems. Dylars become the common currency. Businesses and trade between worlds BOOM! Dylar-money is hailed as the greatest thing to happen in the galaxy for the advancement and benefit of all. Citizens do not understand: They are not reaping the fruits of prosperity and progress. Instead, the treacherous, spider-like Sardon secretly pours vast amounts of profits down a Black Hole and utterly destroys what would help every Citizen in the galaxy.

Legendary Zog reincarnates and deals with Sardon's spirit and minions in various forms throughout time. Neo Zog destroys the Dylar and the Galactic Reserve. The greatest showdown between good and evil, positive and negative, Sardon and Zog, is later. Long after a chaotic age of War between men and women, masterminded by the Sardon. Women gain control of forbidden nuclear weapons, madness continues. Zog's energy returns to the Continuum as the powerful Neo Zog. Decrepit, aged, dead, soulless thing that was the Sardon Chancellor...returns to the material world...as a slick android that resembles a young, pretty, blonde "starlet." She fools all Citizens over galactic Media that she's a real girl. She becomes a popular sensation: singing, dancing, acting in films...*but the cute kid is the Devil!*

Neo Zog battles "Mebby" on the set of the child's new movie, with unbelievable consequences. The actions, reboots, battle-changes, boil down to one hand of the card game: Tonk. But is our hero supposed to win the game, as the fateful hour of 2100 approaches, or lose the game?

Available in e-book and paperback
Find links to purchase at
www.twbpress.com/thecontinuum

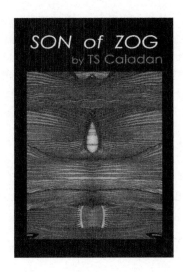

Son of Zog The sequel and second installment of the "Traylogy," is a shorter and to-the-point book. My pen-name was taken from the hero in Book One, artist Tray Caladan, once touched by the power of Zog. In Book Two, I killed myself (character of me) off in the first chapter and left a pregnant wife. Because of my family's actions/spirits in the previous Continuum, the new world reformed to basically a galactic Paradise for 1900 years. Perfection never lasts; the Pendulum swung the other way. The galaxy darkened, went punk/violent/warlike. All Citizens felt the negative vibrations as again the fateful year of 2100 would soon be upon the world.

Tray's son, Sam, is born without a father and into a violent universe that grows darker and deadlier every year. He believes his mother killed his father and turns on her. She's killed and Sam is suspected of the murder. Sam tunes with the vibration of the times and becomes extremely violent. He joins the crazy military.

In 'Son of Zog,' there is actually a lot of humor. The comedy, here and there, of course, is used to offset the wars and murders and madness of a once beautiful galaxy.

Sam discovers his mother did not murder his father and he is on the road to recovery and redemption. The boy becomes a man, almost an immortal, and another version of his father. He inherits his father's (as Neo Zog) gigantic crystal base. Not only does he tap the large crystals for historical knowledge they contain, but he also communicates with his passed-on parents. They tell him of former lifetimes and the important role his family has played in the continuation of the galaxy.

We learn of our history as Sam touches the crystals and sees/feels the ancient past (Atlantis and Egypt). And shocking human origins on Mars, which is what will transpire in Book Three. The sequel concludes with one more card game at End Times of 2100. Will the universe continue?

Available in e-book and paperback
Find links to purchase at
www.twbpress.com/sonofzog

The Cydonian War
by TS Caladan

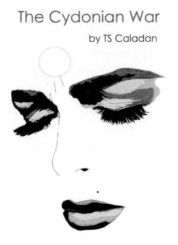

The Cydonian War   Final installment of the "Traylogy" is my White Book. White Space, not the black/emptiness of outer space. What if space, everywhere, was white and filled with limitless energy? *You'd have all the power you could ever use.* Then you discovered your universe, very slowly, was losing its light, energy and power! Goodness was going. Everything, over countless millenniums, was growing dark, cold and empty. It's *universal perfection* lost this time as the bright world slowly morphs into the cosmos of today we're familiar with.

We were Martians, originally, is the theory. We were supermen and superwomen, gods. We could fly, even into space, and we were super-psychic. Masters of (Tesla's) Electro-Magnetic Technology. Mars was known as Shasheer and we were Shasheerans. Central Power Station on the beautiful blue/green, 4th planet was called "Cydonia." Giant Sphinx Face and Pyramid Station were dedicated to my family (Book 2), Father: El. Mother: Jara and holy child: Jar-El. (Similar to Superman story) Shasheeran Utopia will end with the coming Darkness and because of the Sons of Bel, a violent band of rebel anarchists that are exploring new, wild freedoms. Utopia shatters. Rebels take control of Cydonia and change the life-giving Pyramid Fountain of Super Energy into a Weapon of Dark Energy.

El warns others of the corruption on Shasheer and the coming

Universal Darkening, but is ignored. El and Jara put their young child in an escape pod and send him to the safety of the third planet.

To demonstrate their power, Great Weapon is used by the Sons of Bel to **pulverize the 5ᵗʰ planet!** Lilith was even more fantastic and unique than Shasheer and held Shasheeran "Ghosts." Spirits of the ancient Martians were contained within the misty "shells" of innocent creatures on the 5ᵗʰ planet, Lilith. In parallel, one for one. When Bel followers shattered Lilith (in the gap), which will form the Asteroid Belt in far future, they also ended the existence of their own spirit-Ghosts.

The world darkened more. The super force of the Great Explosion ruined Shasheer, *turned it red with poisonous radiation. A wonderful, lush planet was made inhabitable. Billions died.*

The child, Jar-El, less powerful than his godlike parents, still retained incredible abilities and knowledge. He clones himself and builds Atlantis, the world grid, but it pales in comparison to the perfection and power of what once existed back home on Shasheer. In time, the boy grows into a man and finds his new world on Earth has also been infected by evil. It followed him from Mars to Earth. Atlantis is corrupted by rebels and armies of Belia, after thousands of years of a utopia. Jar-El must destroy the little paradise he created so Belia does not control the global stations. Atlantis sinks.

The Earth renews. In time, spirits return. The man builds one more paradise, an even smaller and less potent world grid, centered in Egypt. Same cycles of events must play themselves out. The man must again destroy what he'd built and what he loves.

A Time War takes us back to Mars and to the events at Cydonia with a different conclusion.

Available in e-book and paperback
Find links to purchase at
www.twbpress.com/thecydonianwar

Science-Faction
by TS Caladan

40 stories from the author of the 'Traylogy'

Science-Faction I had written so many short stories that a large book became a two-volume set. Readers can sample stories that range from:

- Three Marilyn Monroes and James Dean in a torrid, film noir classic, just before Pearl Harbor.
- Alternate ending to my Traylogy, a very dark and disturbing, alternate ending.
- A twist on the giant monsters of Japanese movies and add Perry Mason.
- Grey aliens abduct people, but they get addicted to Skittles ("cheesecake").
- NUMBERS oddly appear, visually, over some people's heads. What do they mean?
- Sherlock Holmes tracks down and solves the mystery of: Who is Jack the Ripper?
- Where did (we) the Martians come from? The answer is in: 'Before Shasheer.'
- Is the Earth only a 'Venusian Zoo'? A desperate plea to the 2nd planet.
- A twist on werewolf movies with one particular family and their "curse."
- A twist on zombie movies. A quarantined island of those

infected with "Virus-H."
- 'How Galileo Saved the Life of Captain John Smith.'
- An emotional story I did not write. Aliens wrote it and gave it to me. No one believes me. It's called 'The Prince and the Whipping Post.'

The title of the two-volume set refers to a style of writing I've developed and refined for more than ten years. I don't write Science-Fiction, if you think SF is fantasy. My "fiction" always relates to the real world. I'm expressing statements, political ones, sharp jabs to the corrupt State we're forced to serve and pay tribute. But the ideas, knowledge, secrets, answers, truths, are couched in stories.

"Science-Faction" might describe my fiction the best.

Available in e-book and paperback
Find links to purchase at
www.twbpress.com/sciencefaction

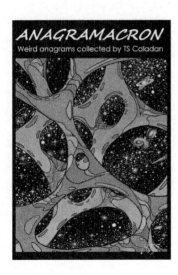

The Anagramacron Possibly the strangest things I've ever seen are "speaking anagrams." Perfect anagrams to words, names, and just about anything. If the rearranged letters are perfect, in other words, every letter formed words...a weird thing happens, on many occasions: The anagrams seem to apply to the subject, whatever is anagrammed. Letters shouldn't do that. In the age of computers and anagram generators, anything typed in and punched, the A.G. spits out every possible combination of rearranged letters. The most sensible words, phrases and complete sentences are listed at the top, instantly.

The entire year of 2006, I used an Anagram Generator and was in utter awe of what appeared in front of my eyes. Treasures! I had to record the phenomenal results. Imagine a real Quija board, "speaking" to you, telling you spot-on information through anagrams with a push of a button! Computers proved the credibility of Speaking Anagrams.

Famous names have a "fate" attached to them. Jim Morrison = Mr. Mojo Risin'. Clint Eastwood = Old West Action. Or words: mother-in-Law = woman Hitler. Why did the ancients revere anagrams, scientists, seers, the royalty of many countries? How did they know back then the high value of special anagrams without the aid of computers? History of anagrams is presented.

The 'Anagramacron' could be the best collection of weird,

funny and freaky anagrams ever assembled. It reads like an encyclopedia. Look up People and Things. You will immediately discover the Power of Anagrams. Mere letters should not do what they do, *but they do!* You'll be amazed.

I am also very proud of the front cover. Six months of work by hand, pencil and ink.

Available in e-book and paperback
Find links to purchase at
www.twbpress.com/anagramacron

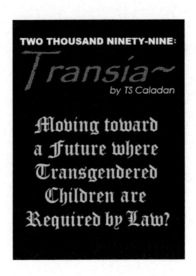

2099 ~ Transia   Have you ever been pissed off about something so intensely, you had to do something about it? What if you found out just about every famous person and celebrity Hollywood, TV or England have ever placed in front of our eyes...was not the sex that they appeared to be? Male and female hormones will do that, taken by the opposite sex. The most masculine men over all Media have been women and the sexist woman have been men! What? Hard to believe, but it's true. A royal tradition for ages. Outsiders have no clue how far the lies and deceptions go of the royalty, the celebrities and almost every famous and promoted person in every field. It might shatter your world and sense of everything if you found out that girls weren't in Playboy...they were in Playgirl. Or what Victoria's Secret really means? You might get pissed.

I wrote the new '1984' in two weeks, *on paper!* During a computer crash. I had to, had no choice and on the evening of the 14th day, after writing like a maniac, I finished a rough/completed version of '2099 – Transia.' What nightmare scenario could I imagine for the end of the 21st Century? How about mandatory transgenders? Everyone had to be *trannies,* and you had to do it to your children, because: It was the LAW! That theme is explored in my Rip Van Winkle story of a man from our time who happens to have been frozen and, unfortunately, wakes up in 2099. 'Transia.'

TS Caladan

Available in paperback only
Find links to purchase at
www.twbpress.com/2099transia

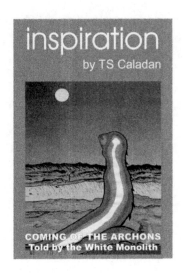

inspiration 'inspiration' was pure fun to write. The story was an experiment. What would I come up with if I simply TOOK OFF? I wasn't sure where I'd go, where the story would take me, but I knew that it would be a marvelous experience...and 'inspiration' turned out even better than expected. Funny. Sexy. Informative. I believe it is the best banter between a human and an android. Can't think of one movie that surpassed it. Emotions/friendships. Jokes, but quality jokes and one-liners. It's a gift. And the story is hot. Why not toss good old-fashioned sex in to spice up the pot?

Plenty of surprises in store as a lowly Company ship is, strangely, permitted to go on an "important" mission to the planet Mercury by the high alien Council. Unprecedented. Earth is nothing in the grand scheme of things. Why send a Company ship to open a sealed, holy Library on Mercury? What's the Council have up their sleeve?

"inspiration" is an anti-Evolution book. The team breaks through computer barriers and the sacred First Book of the Great Library is opened. Human Origin is a massive galactic mystery. First Book shows, in super detail, the pageantry of the human race as it crawled out of primordial Black Goo. The question: "Is the ancient record a documentary and audiences are viewing the truth, or is the Book a grand work of fiction?" is debated endlessly. The question, or answer, of Human Origin causes chaos and, eventually, terrible wars.

Maybe events happen for a reason? The Devil appears OUT of a Black Hole in the center of our galaxy and claims our universe as his domain. There's a surprise waiting for him.

Available in e-book and paperback
Find links to purchase at
www.twbpress.com/inspiration

******** ABOUT THE AUTHOR

Tray Caladan was born Doug Yurchey in Pittsburgh, PA. in 1951 to Rose and Stephen Yurchey. A shy, only-child retreated into his own world and drew pictures. He earned a tennis scholarship to Edinboro State as an art major only to quit and begin the 'Art Trek' gallery. He married a psychic (Katrina) that would forever change his life and send him on a course to solve great mysteries. In 1990-91, he worked as a background cleanup artist on the 'Simpsons.' Tray's important articles, books, videos, radio shows, theories, patent, stories, ideas, games and art can be viewed online. His positive message of a "New Human Genesis" from Mars and ancient technology based on the work of Nikola Tesla permeates his theories and research as well as his "Science Fiction" and life.

Find links to all his e-books and paperbacks at
www.twbpress.com/authortraycaladan.html

TS Caladan

Find links to more stories and more authors at

http://www.twbpress.com
Science Fiction – Supernatural – Horror – Thrillers – & more